Under
the Shadow
of your
Wings

Under the Shadow of your Wings

TEN LENTEN SERMONS ON COVENANT THEMES

CRAIG DOUGLAS ERICKSON

C.S.S. Publishing Co., Inc.

Lima, Ohio

Library of Congress Cataloging-in-Publication Data

Erickson, Craig Douglas, 1948-
 Under the shadow of your wings.

  1. Lenten sermons. 2. Sermons, American. 3. Presbyterian Church (U.S.A.) — Sermons. 4. Presbyterian Church — Sermons. 5. Holy Week sermons. 6. Easter — Sermons. 7. Covenants (Theology) — Sermons. I. Title.
BV4277.E75 1987 252'62   86-28348
ISBN 0-89536-844-7

2.87 2.1T

7803 / ISBN 0-89536-844-7   PRINTED IN U.S.A.

Table of Contents

DEDICATION

To Jeanne Marie,
    who has taught me much about Covenant

and to Michelena,
    a child of the Covenant

How priceless is your love, O God!
    Your people take refuge under the
        shadow of your wings.

                                            Psalm 35 (36):7

Introduction

J. B. Phillips, after completing his paraphrase-translation of the New Testament, likened the task to re-wiring an old house with the electric current on. The same may be said of Covenant Theology, the theme of this collection of Lenten homilies. The Covenant remains a useful concept around which to organize the Bible's expansive message. Surging through its veins is a rich understanding of God and the nature of humankind. Timeless is its sense of the Church of Jesus Christ.

Traditional Covenant Theology stresses three fundamental themes: grace, continuity, and obligation.

Grace. God is a convenanting God. His eternal will is to bring people into life-giving communion with him. Moreover, God's pur pose remains faithful and true, regardless of what humans do. God's grace comes as gift to those who do not deserve it.

Continuity. There is but one Covenant stretching from the beginning of creation to the end of time. This everlasting Covenant has signs of God's intention, e.g. the Rainbow following the flood; circumcision; the Ten Commandments, given to the Hebrews at Sinai; and the sacraments, given to the New Israel by Christ.

Obligation. The Covenant is like a treaty between a benevolent King and his subjects. When the sovereign announces the grace of the covenents, the people are invited to enter into it and to fulfill their side of the treaty obligation. Humanity has definite responsibilities in the Covenant with God, although this is in no way the condition for God's merciful action. God's initiative invites a faithful response. Grace demands obedience![1]

This book is for all Christians. The sermons are especially appropriate for devotional reading during Lent. This book is also for homilists and students of preaching. The first section is included for them, notes on preparing a sermon along with observations on the nature of the homiletical task during Lent and Holy Week.

The author wishes to acknowledge the generous assistance of

those who provided many valuable suggestions in the preparation of this manuscript: Jeanne Marie Huey; Beverle J. Huey; the Rev. James Gaderlund; and Pamela Gaderlund. Appreciation is also due to J. Wilbur Patterson and L. Newton Thurber of the Program Agency of the Presbyterian Church (U.S.A.), who agreed that the use of an unanticipated missionary furlough should be devoted to this purpose. Scripture quotations in this work are from the Revised Standard Version of the Bible, copyrighted 1946, 1952, © 1971, 1973.

Eugene, Oregon
Transfiguration 1986

Part 1.

Effective Serial Preaching During Lent

The Sermon Series: Getting Started

A series is a formidable challenge to the homilist. It is a test of organizational skills, creativity, diversity, and endurance, for having set one's hand to the plow, one cannot then look back. Why attempt a series? The preacher is the immediate beneficiary. A series forces the homilist to do systematic reflection in biblical theology. It is a way of expanding theological horizons. It also stretches and improves homiletical skills.

The series enriches the congregation. It is an effective approach to Bible study. It provides a unifying focus, sustained over several weeks. It is a mnemonic device, around which serious doctrinal teaching may occur.

The great temptation in the introductory sermon is to preview the entire series: "This is where we're going. At this stop, we will see such and such. You will observe that I have done my homework and that you are going to get your money's worth." Such an approach is guaranteed to cure parish insomnia.

Better to view the opening homily as a lure, a sample, a fleeting glimpse that arouses curiosity. The climax is spoiled by revealing all in the opening moments. This is especially true when the series is linked to a season, as is this one. The introduction should create excitement over the spiritual pilgrimage ahead.

The introductory sermon introduces the series topic. It needs to create the sense that a formidable subject is indeed fathomable. It must take the plunge, but then immediately provide bearings. The introductory sermon, then, should provide an enticing preview and a secure footing on unfamiliar terrain.

In the first sermon, the analogy of marriage to the Covenant serves both objectives. It is a fleeting image, which is suggestive of the scope of the series. It provides an orientation for the listeners, most of whom can immediately relate to being married. For Christians, the experience of marriage, despite its ambiguities, remains a viable sign of the promises of God's Covenant.

Series Preaching and the Lectionary

A series drawn from the lectionary is doubly challenging. One must guard against imposing a theme upon a reading, i.e. the using of a text as a pretext. Careful exegesis is a prerequisite. Many potential themes will likely be discarded on the way to discovering that unifying topic that is naturally present in the configuration of texts.

Careful notice of how a lectionary is designed will reveal possibilities for series preaching. Much has been made of the distinction between *lectio continua* and *lectio selecta*. The former refers to the unbroken reading of texts from the same source. For example, one chapter per week is read in succession from Romans, until the entire book is completed. This is an honorable tradition with a long history. Expository preaching according to this pattern would simply expand upon the thematic development present therein. *Lectio selecta* is a more intentional structure, in which readings are selected to complement the progression of the Church Year. This pattern also enjoys a long and honorable tradition.

The distinction between *continua* and *selecta* is somewhat academic. The *continua* approach must initially select the Scripture that is to be covered (hence, few preaching series on Numbers!) The *selecta* method is a recessive pattern in the contemporary lectionaries. They make more frequent use of a pattern that is better described as semi-continuous, which combines principles of both *continua* and *selecta*. For example, the Common Lectionary lists Luke 7:11-17 for one Lord's Day, Luke 7:36—8:3 for the next (a break of nineteen verses). For the next Lord's Day, the lectionary jumps to Luke 9:18-24, and so on. Where the lectionary follows this kind of semi-continuous pattern of text selection, rich possibilities exist for a series of homilies.

The 1983 (CCT) Common Lectionary,[2] from which the texts for this series have been taken, is distinctive for its semi-continuous pattern of Old Testament readings (parent lectionaries had consistently used the Old Testament lesson as a "prop" for the Gospel reading). In the Old Testament track for Lent, Cycle B, the Covenant theme is an intentional one. During Holy Week, the theme is "handed off" to the New Testament readings that mark the establishment of the New Covenant as foretold by the prophets.

Selecting the Series Topic

In selecting the series topic, several considerations should be made.

1. Let the Bible speak its own message. Careful exegesis will determine whether the topic under consideration is naturally unfolded in the lessons. The line between God's Word and the preacher's words is razor thin. Resist the temptation to impose a thematic framework that violates the text. The preacher who rides roughshod over Scripture does so at a great price: credibility.

2. Use a theological dictionary. For example, a series of lessons appear to be related by a common theme of holiness. The theological dictionary's entry on "Sanctification" will quickly determine the possibilities of a well-rounded treatment of the topic in a series. (See Appendices for a bibliography of tools useful in the preparation of the sermon series).

3. Gauge the pastoral need and level of receptivity. A series on worship can be helpful to the parish in the midst of liturgical change. A lengthy series on issues of social justice may "burn out." A lengthy series on prayer may be met with polite ennui. Pastoral sensitivity is the entree to the reception of God's Word.

4. Consult lectionary commentaries. They provide an overview that will suggest possibilities. (See appendices for Bibliography of Lectionary preaching resources.)

5. Consider the framing of the series. No criticism is more stinging than the complaint that the homilist is "on his/her hobbyhorse again." The defensive reaction is that "the congregation must need this emphasis, since they are so resistant to it." Aside from such polemics, it is the preacher's responsibility to provide a well-rounded diet, a representative balance of biblical truth. In selecting the series topic, one must consider what had gone before and what will come after this one. To insure balance, a core checklist of categories may be devised, as for example this one:

1 — *Bible*

2 — *theology and doctrine*

3 — *ethics*

4 — *pastoral*

5 — *liturgy/worship*

6 — *spirituality*

This series on Covenant would fall into category 2; a series on "Ruth" would register in category 1, on "Eucharist" in category 5, and so forth. Over the years, after preaching many series, a rough parity between the categories should begin to emerge.

6. Work well in advance. A lead-time of several months is appropriate for a major series. This will allow for the budgeting of materials and preparation time and enable incubation to occur.

7. Be open to any possibilities. For example, the preacher in reaction against the millennialist preoccupations of a bygone era may unwittingly forfeit an excellent opportunity to preach on eschatology during the Sundays of Christ the King and Advent. The active learner will seize the series as an opportunity to venture out, to explore new areas of learning. That you "don't know anything about a topic" should not be an excuse to avoid it. Remember: the homilist's excitement over new discoveries will likely be contagious.

The Length of the Sermon Series

In addition to the topic itself, other factors influence the length of the series.

Pastoral Considerations. The preacher's calling is to to serve the people of God. Their needs, level of interest, and span of concentration are all factors to consider in setting the length of the series.

Lectionary. As previously noted, the semi-continuous lectionary readings provide rich possibilities for series preaching. For example, a lectionary that devotes four Lord's Days to Colossians or three Lord's Days to Ruth suggests obvious themes and lengths.

Church Year. Advent, Lent, and Eastertide lend themselves to series preaching. The homily series highlights these seasons as intensified periods of Christian growth. Note that the climax of Lent is Easter; of Eastertide, Pentecost; of Advent, Christmas. The First Sundays after Christmas or Easter, low days in the Church Year, are anti-climactic days on which to begin or end a series. A series during Advent may appropriately include Christ the King.

Ability. Series preaching may be compared to mountain climbing. You master the ropes on the smaller peaks, where the risks are minimal. Only when you have the skills under your belt do you tackle a Mount Rainier, confident that you are up to a larger undertaking. Mountain climbing is most perilous when the participants are fatigued. Series preaching must be plotted carefully. so that preacher and congregation do not become exhausted en route.

Series preaching puts the homilist under pressure. Consequently, to succeed at it, one must have stamina, a rare quality in the inexperienced preacher. The building blocks of endurance are: more modest goals (two or three-part series at most) and regular (preferably weekly) preaching experience. Gradually, one's repertoire of biblical and theological knowledge expands, accompanied by a growing efficiency in preparation. Only then should the homilist attempt a major series of four to eight sermons, ever-mindful of the many hazards that can thwart the effort, even for the most experienced climbers.

Outlining the Series

From the standpoint of preparation, there is one significant advantage to series preaching. It is more economical. Because the background reading and reflection applies not just to one sermon but to several, there is an efficiency of preparation. A rough schematic for the entire series will unfold almost as easily as the outline of an individual homily.

    Outlining the series is like planning a trip. The objective is to see what there is to see. At the same time, this should be done efficiently. Most of all, you want to avoid dead-ends, such as arriving at the ferry slip only to discover that the boats don't operate that month.

    The outline is a way of calculating the cost, of seeing ahead of time whether or not the series will work. It should be done far in advance, to allow for incubation time. The working outline for this series appears below.

Day/Week of Church Year	Theme	Sign	Preaching Text
Ash Wednesday	A Covenant of Mercy	Ashes, sign of cross, penance	Joel 2:1-2, 12-17a
Lent 1	A Covenant extending to all of Creation	Rainbow	Genesis 9:8-17
Lent 2	The faith response to God's initiative	Abraham, Sarah, Isaac; circumcision, Baptism	Genesis 17:1-19
Lent 3	A Covenant of Law	Ten Commandments	Exodus 20:1-17
Lent 4	A Gospel Covenant	(Hebrew restoration from exile in Babylon)	2 Chronicles 36:14-23
Lent 5	An interiorized Covenant	(Spirit)	Jeremiah 31:31-34
Palm/Passion Sunday	The Covenant's demand: The way of the cross.	Baptism	Isaiah 50:4-9a/ Philippians 2:5-11
Holy (Maundy) Thursday	The Covenant memorial	Passover/Eucharist Christ's blood shed	Exodus 24:3-8; 1 Corinthians 10:16-17
Good Friday	The Covenant established	Cross	Isaiah 52:13—53:12
Easter Day	The Covenant ratified and its promise: The New Life in Christ.	garments, Baptism	Ezekiel 36:24-28

Sustaining the Series

    The homilist must calculate how to sustain the series. The effectiveness of the sermon series will be diminished if listeners sense a sameness to each unit. An intentional variation of styles is even more critical in series preaching, so that the parish does not grow weary of the topic. The longer the series, the more internal variety will be needed. The series should plan the use of more than one of the basic homiletical forms, which include:

1. **Expository.** A running commentary on the biblical text (example: sermon for Lent 2).

2. **Thematic.** A central idea with a progressive development, usually two to three points, and a climax (example: sermon for Lent 3).

3. **Faceting.** One basic truth is examined from several perspectives. The basic truth may be repeated as a leitmotiv, gaining depth and power with each occurrence (example: sermon for Palm/Passion Sunday).

4. **Creative.** Any of various, freely-composed styles, e.g. dramatic monologues, epistolary, narrative, parables, etc. (example: sermon for Lent 5).

The homily "Written Upon Their Hearts" is the rondo in this series. Its parabolic style springs from the anthropopathism[3] of the text from Jeremiah. It is an impressionistic treatment of the New Covenant theme, using childhood and adolescent developmental patterns as an analogy for Israel's development of Covenant Theology. The New Covenant that Jeremiah envisioned will change humankind's motivation to obey God's Law.

The Lenten Pilgrimage

There is a common theme running through much of the world's great literature, namely: The outer journey is the occasion for an inner pilgrimage. The motif is a pervasive one. It is what the wily Odysseus has in common with Conrad's Marlow *(Heart of Darkness)*, what links Melville's "Captain Ahab" with Hemingway's "Old Man." In literature, characters who outwardly participate in an adventure, simultaneously undergo an inner transformation. They change, in some cases for the better, in some for the worse, but in all cases, they emerge as different persons. That is why their stories live on.

This literary motif helps us to grasp the movement of the yearly Lenten pilgrimage. The liturgies of Lent correspond to the outer journey that becomes the occasion for an inner transformation.

The sermons in this book trace the theme of the Covenant. Indeed, it is a Grand Tour of the Covenant and its signs, tracing them across the ages. With the arrival of the pilgrimage at the gates of the holy city of Jerusalem, expectations are intensified. Here will be staged the central events of the Christian faith.

On the Lenten pilgrimage, the preacher serves as spiritual guide. His or her responsibility is to escort the pilgrims from "sight" to "sight," offering reflections at the appropriate junctures. The guide's sole objective is to bring the pilgrim into an encounter with the saving mystery of Christ, therein to be renewed by the power of the Holy Spirit.

Effective preaching complements the liturgy. This is especially true during Holy Week. The preaching should support the liturgy and be supported by it. It must not ignore it, fight it, or dominate it.

The services of Holy Week function as a unit, much like a four-act play. Each "act" unfolds another dimension of the Mystery. Each "act' exits the stage leaving a heightened sense of anticipation about what will follow.

The Palm Sunday/Passion Sunday celebration opens on a festive note with the procession of palms. But his triumphalism is not what it appears. He who is acclaimed Messiah with shouts of "Hosanna," is actually a Suffering Servant. His kingdom is not of this world. The preacher's task is to re-orient the triumphalistic acclamations of "Hosanna" to the stark reality of the Cross.

The Palm Sunday sermon should be a clarion call to discipleship. Those who would follow this Messiah must be prepared to accept the cost, as Christ said: "Take up your cross and follow me." Consequently, Palm Sunday is an appropriate occasion to reflect upon the meaning of the sacraments, and, in particular, baptism, which is the occasion for turning from the old way to follow the new.

Following the sermon is the reading of the Passion narrative, which gives this day its alternate name of Passion Sunday. The

Lord's Supper on this day is mindful of Jesus' challenge to his disciples:

Are you able to drink the cup that I drink, or to be baptized with the baptism with which I am baptized? Mark 10:38

As the curtain falls on Act 1, the orientation is decisive. Holy Week will lead the pilgrim along a path of servanthood, suffering, and death — as a necessary prelude to exaltation. The Way of the Cross, the outer journey, will be the occasion for an inner transformation. That's why the story of the Christ lives on!

Overtones: Holy (Maundy) Thursday

Why is this night different from all other nights? The liturgy for Holy Thursday is rich in Jewish overtones. The lessons refer to the Passover. The Psalmody is excerpted from the Hallel (the so-called "Egyptian Hallel," read during the Haggadah (Psalms 112 [113]-117 [118]). The humble act of footwashing hearkens back to the ritual ablutions that accompanied the typical Jewish meal in Jesus' time. The Eucharistic act is doubly mindful of its origins in Jewish table rituals (Berakah) and the Passover context of the Last Supper. The Passover holds a dominant influence on the liturgy for Holy Thursday. It establishes its tone as one of warm, effusive praise to God. Like the Passover, Holy Thursday is brimming with light and hope, sublimely confident that the Lord who has gloriously triumphed will remember his people.

The preaching should reflect the Jewish overtones of the liturgy. The homilist should be thoroughly familiar with the Haggadah, so that illustrative references may be drawn from it. The sermon may appropriately focus on some aspect of Eucharistic theology, celebrating with the liturgy, the institution of the memorial of our redemption.

The liturgy for Holy Thursday differs from the Passover in one important respect. While the Seder is a celebration that moves from darkness to light, the Maundy Thursday liturgy ends in darkness. The altar-table has been stripped bare. The stage is now set for the most solemn act of Holy Week, the focus of which is the cross of Christ.

Joining in the Prayer

Do worship leaders worship? The question sounds superfluous. However, many of them would admit that their experience of worship is vulnerable to concerns over liturgical flow, logistics, and execution. During Holy Week, such preoccupations are accentuated. The solo pastor may be faced with four to five occasions for preaching, all within the context of extraordinary liturgies. In order to enter into the prayer of Holy Week, the preacher must make special provisions.

The weekdays following the fourth and fifth Sundays in Lent should be devoted solely to the preparation of sermons for Holy Week. The congregation needs to understand that this preparatory period is crucial to its life. Committee meetings, parish conflicts, visitations, and broken mimeograph machines will all have to wait. A working stay at a monastery or other hideaway where the phone doesn't ring is well justified during these weeks. Centering silence is an absolute necessity to responsible preparation.

The goal for the homilist is to arrive at Palm/Passion Sunday with the Holy Week sermons virtually completed. This will enable him or her to enter into the experience of Holy Week with a minimum of *angst*. With sermons in hand, the preacher will be able to join fully in the prayer of Holy Week, free to meditate on God's Word without being preoccupied with sermonic applications, able to center in the prayerful contemplation of the death and resurrection of Christ.

The congregation is poorly served by a homilist who shows the fatigue of preparation. The homiletical task is not an easy one — everyone knows that. Yet the rules of the game forbid a preacher from showing it.

Because of this, the preacher must conserve every spare ounce of energy during the last weeks of Lent. Forget about "hours logged in the office." If you have to spend Holy Thursday or Good Friday out walking a trail so that your spirit is pure and fresh for the liturgy that day, do it! Do whatever it takes to be alive, alert, unharried, fresh, sharp, buoyant, at peace, radiant.

The preacher's professional responsibility is to resonate with the prayer of the Holy Week liturgies. The people of God deserve no less — that's why they have graced you with ordination. Your preaching and worship leadership will be most effective when it is engaged with your spirit. In that way will you be an instrument of the ministry of the Holy Spirit.

From Darkness to Light: The Resurrection of Our Lord

Writer's block. It happens to the best of them. "The Easter sermon. It's supposed to be my best sermon of the year. Yet, all my thoughts sound trivial. What can I possibly say about the Resurrection? It's so overwhelming. Six choirs on deck for Easter Sunday! That's really going to put the squeeze on my 'best sermon of the year.' "

Professional writers say there's no such thing as writer's block. It's all in your head. Nonetheless, the creative forces may need to be freed up by some reality therapy.

1. Easter preaching is seldom unhindered. The fluke snow that forced the cancellation of the Palm Sunday processional has now melted. In its wake, a Gulf front has moved in with the first warm, muggy weather of the spring, making everyone feel less than comfortable. Widow Smith, who tried valiantly to hang on until Easter, has conveniently scheduled her funeral for the day after. Dozens of children who haven't set foot in your sanctuary in a year are out at the Mall being outfitted in Easter finery, so they can fidget and squirm through the liturgy in style. Invariably, at Easter, factors beyond anyone's control encroach upon the homilist.

2. Ferret out the unrealistic expectations that you place upon yourself. There is no reason to expect that your Easter homily will be significantly better than your normal output. Keep in mind that preaching gets a tremendous boost from the liturgies of Easter. Even if it's not your best sermon, the liturgy, if done up right, will cover for you. God's people will still have celebrated the Resurrection, joy will be abundant, the cosmos reaffirmed. The expectation that you can say something to transform Christmas-and-Easter attenders into "regulars" is likely to tempt you to scold. Resist this. Let the Holy Spirit prompt those people into deeper levels of church commitment. Simply be thankful that they are there.

3. Explore other possibilities for preaching texts. While the lectionary is an excellent discipline, it can paralyze the preacher on Easter when the readings focus on a very dense theme: the Resurrection of Christ. For the preacher who is intimidated by so formidable a topic, there is an alternative method of theological reflection that has great integrity.

Theological topics do not exist in isolation. They impinge upon and interact with other themes. It is a legitimate method to approach the Resurrection via the themes that interact with it. Since the Resurrection lies at the heart of Christian doctrine and its influence is so pervasive, you can pick almost any other theological theme and develop it *in the light of the Resurrection.* You would thereby grasp a sense of the whole inductively. Will you have given an exhaustive treatment of the Resurrection? Of course not. You are only covering one chapter. Leave chapter two for next year, and so forth.

The Easter sermon in this book employs this method. Departing from the lectionary, it is based on a lesson that is borrowed from the Paschal Vigil readings. It explores the Resurrection via the theme of the new life in Christ.

4. A final point. Know what food to bring to the party. Easter is a day for milk and honey. Because on this day Christians are bidden to laugh at death, the sermon may appropriately make use of humor. Canned humor is out, though. That is a curse of much modern preaching, for it sends people home with something other than that for which they came. Pulpit humor graciously senses its place. It is situational, humorous only within that context. It is not distracting to the progression of thought in the sermon. It deflects nothing from the glory of God.

The Easter homily, then, must not be too heavy, too long, or too rational. Remember: On this day, nothing is more profound than the people's ALLELUIA!

Part 2.

A Lenten Preaching Series

Ash Wednesday

Scenes From a Marriage

Signs: Ashes, Sign of the Cross, Penance

Scripture:
*Joel 2:1-2, 12-17a
Psalm 50 [51]:1-12
2 Corinthians 5:20b—6:2 [3-10]
Saint Matthew 6:1-6, 16-21[4]

How incongruous to talk about marriage on this solemn Day of Ashes. Marriage evokes images of life and joy and growth, perhaps even of youthful, starry-eyed wonder. But this is a day about dying. It's a day of sober realism and human limitations. It's a day that begins a season of denial, of fasting, and repentance. How incongruous to bring up marriage on this day.

But then, every marriage has its moments. There's not one that doesn't have its darker side, when the "union made in heaven" is all-too-painfully aware of feet mired in clay. You can hardly think of a marriage that hasn't at some point needed help. The agony of marriage in our time supports one sociologist's description of marriage as "a state of tragic tension fraught with difficulties."[5]

It is this perspective that predominates in the early 1970's film "Scenes from a Marriage," by the brilliant Swedish director, Ingmar Bergman. As in every Bergman film, there is in this one an intense level of interaction. The protagonists, a husband and wife, engage in dialogue that is open and frank — brutally frank at times. They are articulate about their deepest needs, fears, and disappointments — so articulate, in fact, that one wonders who will be left to pick up the pieces.

The genius of Bergman's screenplay lies in his ability to show how otherwise desirable virtues can be destructive to human relationships. Open communication? Sure. That's what you want in a marriage. But in Bergman's film, it provokes a defensive hostility that causes the marriage to unravel. How about "being in touch with one's own needs"? Again, essential to a healthy marriage. But in Bergman's characters, it degenerates into self-centeredness. Sexual attraction? This is also nice to have in a marriage, to say the least. But there's a darker side to these drives, which are ever so easily sullied by the human proclivity to dominance and manipulation.

"Scenes from a Marriage" is a tragedy in the classic sense, for Bergman's husband and wife characters are fatally flawed. They lack that which alone keeps virtues from becoming something other than virtues. They lack grace. Without grace, the best of human intentions becomes tragically disoriented. It is grace that keeps a tragic tension from becoming a *destructive* tension. It is grace that enables a marriage to survive.

The Covenant is a kind of marriage between God and His people. It is a marriage that has survived over the ages because God possesses an inexhaustible reservoir of grace. No matter what humans do, even those who have entered into this marriage through baptism, God remains faithful and true. He continues to give himself through a promise that is always there. God's eternal will, to bring people into life-giving communion with him, remains unchanged.

Ash Wednesday is a little scene from this marriage. It is not a pretty scene. It is a dramatic one. The symbol of signing the cross on the forehead in ashes is a poignant statement. It says:

- *I am not God. I am a human being.*
- *I am going to die.*
- *I desperately need God's mercy and grace in my life.*

Now here is some very straightforward communication,

which this marriage and all marriages must have. Here is an articulation of inmost needs, which is preeminently healthy and fair in a marriage. Here is a confession of frailty and weakness, which a marriage must have in order to invite a saving response.

This Ash Wednesday "scene from a marriage" highlights the one key ingredient that keeps all of us from being "burned up by God's fury." In fact, it is the very quality that makes this marriage an experience of salvation, namely: *the abundant, endless, always-extended, never-failing mercy of God.* That's what makes this marriage so wonderful. That's why the church has always held it up as a model for human marriages, so that a "tragic tension fraught with difficulties" might be transformed into a sacrament of God's love and mercy, that is to say, into the adventure of a lifetime.

The prophet Joel, in lines that can scarcely contain his excitement, is saying exactly that:

> *"Yet even now," says the LORD,*
> *"return to me with all your heart,*
> *with fasting, with weeping, and with mourning;*
> *and rend your hearts and not your garments."*
> *Return to the LORD, your God,*
> *for he is gracious and merciful,*
> *slow to anger, and abounding in steadfast love . . .*

Joel 2:12-13

How can you go wrong with God's mercy? Here, under the shadow of his wings, the defenses we have so elaborately erected everywhere around us can only melt away. Here we are loved, welcomed and accepted. Here we are forgiven, healed and restored to newness of life.

It is the Covenant, founded upon God's mercy, that makes Ash Wednesday the day that it is. Today you needn't worry about open communication — this marriage has got it. You can forget the myth that a display of weakness and vulnerability is risky business, for in this marriage, there is one who is more deeply in touch with your needs than you yourself are. Today you need not worry about putting your best foot forward. For when you share in this marriage, you need not fear that which can paralyze any marriage: rejection.

This Day of Ashes, the outward symbols of which speak of sin and death, of repentance and finitude, this day, then is really a celebration of God's open-ended Covenant with us, his people, his betrothed. The Good News is that there is no sin, no confession, no shortcoming, no inadequacy that is not matched by the abundance of God's mercy. That's what the Covenant is: a context that invites openness! It's a marriage that promises acceptance and healing. It's a pilgrimage that delivers us from death unto life!

Lent 1

Steadfast and Faithful

Signs: Rainbow, Baptism, Eucharist

Scripture:
*Genesis 9:8-17
Psalm 24 [25]:1-10
*1 Peter 3:18-22
Saint Mark 1:9-15

"When the (rain)bow is in the clouds, I will look upon it and remember the everlasting covenant between God and every living creature of all flesh that is upon the earth." God said to Noah, "This is the sign of the covenant which I have established between me and all flesh that is upon the earth."

Genesis 9:16-17

God's Covenant of mercy extends to all Creation.

Noah's flood was no ordinary flood. According to the Bible, its distinguishing feature was *not* that it rained for forty days and forty nights. The distinctive feature of this flood is mentioned, almost in passing, in Genesis 7:11: "on that day all the fountains of the great deep burst forth."

What are the fountains of the great deep? The writers of the Old Testament followed the conventional wisdom of the day in assuming that the universe had three stories: heaven, earth, and the underworld. It was believed that water surrounded earth, above and below. The firmament, spread above earth like a huge dome, was thought to be the floor of a heavenly ocean, above which was the dwelling place of the gods. The firmament was supported by pillars and sunk into the subterranean waters. In the depths of these waters was believed to be Sheol, the Kingdom of the Dead. The

Psalmist betrays this worldview in writing:

> *Thou didst set the earth on its foundations,*
> *so that it should never be shaken.*
> *Thou didst cover it with the deep as with a garment;*
> *the waters stood above the mountains.*
> *At thy rebuke they fled;*
> *at the sound of thy thunder they took to flight.*
> *The mountains rose, the valleys sank down to the place*
> *which thou didst appoint for them.*
> *Thou didst set a bound which they should not pass,*
> *so that they might not again cover the earth.*

Psalm 103 (104):5-9

The Old Testament writers believed that they lived in a fragile envelope, one surrounded on all sides by water, the waters of Chaos. (Genesis 7:11) For this reason, Noah's Flood was more than just a flood. It was a flood that threatened to destroy the earth forever. It was a flood that threatened to return earth to its pre-creation state. Noah's Flood was the event when the world was very nearly swallowed up by Chaos.

The story of the Flood is widespread in ancient literature. Is there some historical basis to it? After all, fossils of sea life have turned up in some rather unusual places, such as the Great Plains. A world-wide cataclysmic flood, such as the Bible describes, has prompted many to look to geology for verification.

Scientists who theorize about the early history of the earth often focus on cataclysmic events, spread out through the 2-3 billion years of its existence. Some predict that the Earth "will again collide with an asteroid large enough to cause mass extinctions, as probably happened 65 million years ago, when the dinosaurs vanished."[6]

Others theorize that the poles of planet Earth at one time may have existed along what is presently the equator. A celestial body moving in proximity to Earth exerted a massive gravitational pull upon our planet, causing it to rotate its axis ninety degrees — a cataclysmic event that would certainly have precipitated a massive dislocation of water.

However, no direct scientific evidence exists for a worldwide flood. All that science is able to establish is that the early history of our planet was a violent and turbulent one.

The eruption of Mount Saint Helens was just a little reminder of that.[7] Of course, that eruption was a mere firecracker compared to that of Krakatoa in Indonesia in 1883. The explosion of 27 August that year produced a sound that was heard clear across the Indian Ocean in Malagasy, off of the eastern coast of Africa, some 3,000 miles away. Krakatoa produced an ocean tidal wave that was fifty feet high, destroying coastal villages and settlements for hundreds of miles around, killing some 36,000 people. The disturbance of oceanic waters was noted as far away as the English Channel (11,040 miles distant). In addition, Krakatoa modified global weather patterns. In the United States, 1883 was the so-called "Year of No Summer." Snow fell in the northern states in July and August. Crop failures were widespread.

Could Noah's Flood have been caused by a volcano, or meteorite, or a warming trend and the melting of the polar ice caps? Speculation will not get us very far. Of one thing we can be sure: the biblical writers had no idea that the earth was a sphere, much less one that had a circumference of some 25,000 miles. What may have seemed like the whole world to them, was probably only a small portion of it.

The story of the Flood is less important for its scientific details (or lack thereof) than for its religious message. When we see how the biblical writers cast the story, its significance becomes clear.

1. The biblical version of the Flood, unlike other versions, affirms the goodness of God's creation, the theme on which Genesis opens. When natural catastrophies occur, they often raise doubts about God's Covenant with creation, a Covenant otherwise taken for granted. But the Bible affirms that,

despite temporary appearances to the contrary, God continues to look favorably upon Creation. He still marvels at his handiwork, pausing to say: "That's good!"

2. The biblical account of Noah's Flood also demonstrates in a vivid way that God is not interested in the destruction of our planet but is committed to its redemption. God is one who is active on the stage of history, and not in a capricious way. His movement is purposeful.

3. The story of the Flood is told in such a way as to exult in the orderliness and dependability of God's creation. For a generation that regards such things as Space Shuttle flights as routine, the orderliness of God's creation is something that is merely assumed.[2]

Indeed, the scientific worldview is so persuasive that many do not sense the need to look beyond it for explanations of causality. But the Bible teaches that the "regularities of nature, which moderns have rationalized into 'laws', are at bottom expressions of the faithfulness of God, upon which all rely."[9]

Noah's Flood was terrifying to the ancients because it introduced the prospect of natural laws being overturned. The Covenant that is signed by the rainbow is God's eternal promise to uphold the natural order. There is just no way that the good Lord is going to suspend the laws of gravity, even for one second. Nor do we have to worry about waking up tomorrow and discovering that osmosis is inoperative. We can count on water reaching its greatest density at thirty-nine degrees Fahrenheit, not thirty-two, a phenomenon that makes life as we know it possible. The thought of living in a world where arbitrary suspensions of natural laws periodically occur at the whim of the gods is a frightening one. In such a world, it would be impossible to affirm God's goodness. Purpose and order in creation make it possible to affirm purpose and order in our lives.

The biblical story of the Flood is a bold statement that,

despite the occurrences of natural catastrophies, God has agreed to abide by his natural laws. God is a God of order. To believe otherwise is to court religious superstition and fear. The pervasive presence of order in God's creation leads us to another consideration: the problem of evil. Theologian George S. Hendry writes:

> The presence of evil in a world that was created by a good God and was pronounced good at its creation is a sore trial for faith, and it presents a problem to which no one has found the solution. But one thing may be said: the disorder in the world, which is the cause of so much suffering, becomes problematical only because it stands out from the order, which is the cause of well-being. It is the pervasive presence of order in the structure and workings of the world that throws the fact of disorder into relief; it is the exception to the rule, if not the exception that proves the rule . . .

It does not follow, continues Hendry, that we should seek to console victims of cancer by telling them that most of their fellow human beings are not afflicted by it. "But the fact remains that if there is a problem of evil, there is also a problem of good, and one cannot be isolated from the other.[10]

The Rainbow Covenant is God's promise to uphold an orderly universe, governed by natural laws.

4. Lastly, the Flood story as we have it in the Bible squeezes superstition out of the religious picture. Other ancient religions continued to dally under the illusion that religion could produce or prevent natural phenomena. They manufactured elaborate myths to explain the recurrence of its seasons. They developed intricate rituals in an attempt to control nature.

In the story of Noah, we see the Hebrew faith turning its back on all of that. The Bible does not view religious faith as the key to the mysteries of nature. The Bible proclaims nature as a clue to the Mystery that transcends nature.[11]

The consequences of this insight have been far-reaching. Because our religious tradition views nature not as a hostile force to be feared but as a sphere that is filled with God's presence and God's goodness, it has encouraged the free study and exploration of nature. Noah's Covenant inspired our religious tradition to view nature as a realm in which God is kindly disposed toward humanity.

The belief in the goodness of creation was a tremendous religious breakthrough. It made possible the rise of the modern sciences and their accompanying technological benefits. Granted, certain religious figures may have tried to block scientific advances. For example, Copernicus hardly endeared himself to the bishops when he suggested that astronomical calculations could be more accurate if it were assumed that the earth revolved around the sun. Nor was Charles Darwin ever nominated for Protestant Layman of the Year. Nonetheless, the Judeo-Christian tradition and its Rainbow Covenant have provided an underlying intellectual climate within which the modern sciences have had room to flourish. The Rainbow Covenant was a religious breakthrough of the first order that continues to pay rich dividends for humanity, thousands of years later.

That's what the biblical writers did with the Flood story. However, in marveling at the brilliance of their insight, we must not forget that in all of this there has been a trade-off. Our Judeo-Christian tradition, while it has freed mankind from a superstitious view of nature, has achieved this at the expense of divorcing religion from nature. Consequently, Western, technological society has been alienated from nature. The modern perception views nature as an object to subdue, something over which human beings are to have mastery. Indeed, the problem today is that nature has replaced creation. Scientism has erased God's footprints!

Moreover, the very insight that has freed us for scientific endeavors, bringing many blessings, has also brought a curse: *an environmental crisis of the first order.* The fact of this crisis is not altered by politicians' unwillingness to enforce or enact environmental regulations. A technological culture without adequate religious restraints must have legal restraints to insure that we will not poison ourselves and bequeathe to future generations an inhospitable environment. This is why our Prayers of the People routinely contain a petition for the natural order: "For the good earth which God has given us, and for the wisdom and will to conserve it, let us pray to the Lord: LORD, HAVE MERCY" (BCP).

A covenant is not just a one-way gesture from God to us. It involves a return obligation on our part as well. To enter into God's Rainbow Covenant, we must commit ourselves as faithful stewards of God's creation, to pray and to work for the wisdom and the will to conserve the good earth which God has given us.

God has committed himself to the natural order. Our part of the bargain is to covenant to work *for* God's creation, not against it, to work *with* the Creator, in order to bring creation unto perfection. Baptism marks this aspect of the Covenant. It commits us to environmental awareness and responsibility.

If through Baptism we enter God's Covenant, it is in the Eucharist that this Covenant is renewed. As a priestly community we offer, at the Lord's Table, simple gifts of bread and wine, signs of the goodness of God's creation. With them our prayers are lifted up: "Lord, God, transform your whole Creation by the Mystery of your Divine Word! Bring us to the fullness of your Kingdom. Come, Lord, Jesus."

The Rainbow Covenant is God's invitation to look at the world and all that is therein through the eyes of the Creator!

Come! Eat! Share in the feast of God's goodness.

Lent 2

Believing Against Hope

Signs: Circumcision and Baptism

Scripture:
**Genesis 17:1-10, 15-19
*Psalm 104 [105]:1-11
*Romans 4:16-25
Saint Mark 8:31-38

Part A: The Covenant: God's Initiative

*Genesis 17:1-8 — When Abram was ninety-nine years old
the Lord appeared to Abram, and said to him, "I am God
Almighty (El Shaddai); walk before me, and be blameless.
And I will make my covenant between me and you, and will
multiply you exceedingly." Then Abram fell on his face; and
God said to him, "Behold, my covenant is with you, and you
shall be the father of a multitude of nations. No longer shall
your name be Abram (meaning: exalted father), but your
name shall be Abraham (meaning: father of a multitude); for
I have made you the father of a multitude of nations. I will
make you exceedingly fruitful; and I will make nations of
you, and kings shall come forth from you. And I will establish my covenant between me and you and your descendants
after you. And I will give to you, and to your descendants
after you throughout their generations for an everlasting
covenant, to be God to you and to your descendants after
you, the land of your sojournings, all the land of Canaan,
for an everlasting possession; and I will be their God."*

The Covenant made with Noah, involving all of creation,
is now going to be particularized. It will involve a particular

race, a particular nation, and a particular couple, Abraham and Sarah, who just happen to be both aged and barren (or, as Saint Paul puts it, "as good as dead"!) Why does the LORD wish to establish this relationship with Abraham? It is in God's nature that something that is vague and amorphous should take on definition. Therefore God would transform an uncertain disorder into a relationship that will be wholesome for Abraham and his descendents. God chooses Israel as a special object of his grace.

What a marvelous thing to be special, to be chosen. The heart of the child on the playground beats wildly when among the first to be "chosen up" for a side. Similarly, that promotion, that proposal of marriage, that letter that begins with "Congratulations!", such rare and special moments in life evoke a natural response: "At last, I am *recognized*. My worth is acknowledged. People know that I *am* somebody."

By contrast, when God chooses Abraham, none of this is present. There is no rhyme nor reason why Abraham should have been selected over some other wandering Aramean. The God of Mystery simply selects him, not for anything he has done, nor because he deserved the honor. Just because. That's how God works. Not according to human merit, but according to divine mercy.

Nevertheless, for the Hebrews, this is a marvelous moment. "Behold, my covenant is with you . . ." To be chosen! To be on God's side! Israel is now off on the adventure of a lifetime. A special relationship with the LORD means that she can now exist with a special hope. The Covenant gives to Israel a unique identity, a special vocation among the nations. Now she will belong to God, and God will belong to her.

Genesis 17:7 — "I will establish my covenant between me and you and your descendants after you throughout their generations for an everlasting covenant, to be God to you and to your descendants after you."

With these words, everything falls into place for Israel. That is exactly what a relationship with God does. If you're wondering what life is all about, let God unscramble the mystery for you. If you aren't sure who you really are, let God reveal a unique and precious person. If you're separated and cut off, let God bring you home. If you're confused about what you're supposed to be doing in life, let God give it definition. The encounter with God is life-transforming. It alters your whole sense of who you are. That's why Abram and Sarai emerge from the Covenant-making with new names. They will never again be the same.

"I will establish my covenant . . . to be God to you and to your descendants after you."

These words are not just addressed to Abraham. They're also addressed to us! Four thousand years later, the Covenant is still there, extended for us!

Not so fast! That's almost too good to be true. There must be a catch!

There *is* a catch. To be chosen by God means blessings and privileges for sure. But there are also responsibilities. In the Covenant with Noah, God promised to uphold the natural order, to keep forever the waters of Chaos from destroying Creation. God also gave permission to humankind to eat meat, although it must be bloodless. (Genesis 9:1-5) But along with new privileges went some new responsibilities. Humankind must now be a steward of God's creation. For example, human beings are not to shed blood wantonly, especially the blood of other human beings. (Genesis 9:6) Humanity is charged to respect and to take care of God's creation.

In the Covenant with Abraham, there is a similar linkage of blessings and responsibilities. The blessings are national identity, a land in which to live, and offspring more numerous than the stars of the heavens. (Genesis 15:5) What are Israel's responsibilities?

Part B: Circumcision and Baptism

Genesis 17:9-10 — And God said to Abraham, "As for you, you shall keep my covenant, you and your descendants after you throughout their generations. This is my covenant which you shall keep, between me and you and your descendants after you: Every male among you shall be circumcised."

Circumcision is to be the sign or brand of membership in the Covenant community. Modern medical studies conclude that, from an hygienic viewpoint, there are neither advantages nor disadvantages to the practice of circumcision. So then, is circumcision a throwback to primitive religion, in which the body is scarred to signify membership in the tribe? Perhaps. And wouldn't you agree that mature religion has to do with spirit, not matter?

Judeo-Christian faith is more than a headtrip. We don't just think and talk about our faith. We *act* upon it. We use symbols, not only to show that we mean business, but also to effect what we symbolize.

The wedding ritual illustrates this. From a legal standpoint, there is only one thing necessary to getting married: mutual consent before witnesses, and having the proper signatures in the proper slots on the marriage license. That's all that's required. So then why do we make nervous brides and grooms stand up in front of everyone and with sweaty palms stammer through their vows? Is it to haze them? Hardly. The ritual is necessary to the bonding. You can't just *think* about your commitments in life. You have to *demonstrate* them, and thereby enact them. Circumcision did that for the Hebrews. It demonstrated belonging to the Covenant in a way that actually accomplished it.

Circumcision did not have an uncontroversial place in Jewish history. Any ritual can degenerate into ritual*ism*. None are immune. It was inevitable that circumcision would for many become just a formality. And it was inevitable, once this had happened, that a Hebrew prophet would burst onto the stage with a startling message: "Empty rituals are an offense to God! True circumcision is a matter of the heart, not the flesh. What really counts is not marking your body, but yielding your complete devotion to God. If circumcision genuinely expresses that, fine. But if it doesn't, watch out! God despises formalities, especially liturgical ones."

For Christians, thanks to the Apostle Paul (Acts 15:1-5), circumcision is no longer an issue. So why belabor it? Answer: Because circumcision is regarded as the forerunner of Baptism. (Colossians 2:11-13) Despite all the New Testament polemic against circumcision, it still holds a special place in Christian theology as a prototype for Baptism. Circumcision is to the Old Covenant what Baptism is to the New Covenant.

So if it's possible that circumcision can become an empty ritual, then maybe it's also possible that Baptism runs a similar risk. The sacraments are no guarantee of entrance into the Promised Land. (1 Corinthians 10) That's why the church insists upon pastoral discretion in administering the sacrament. Baptism is not a magical act that somehow works independently of faith and apart from the nurturing community of the church.

Question from the back row: If faith is necessary to Baptism, then why is it that the church baptizes infants, who are incapable of faith as we know it? Excellent question.

The church baptizes the infants of believers as a sign of the covenant promise "to you and your descendants after you throughout their generations for an everlasting covenant." (Genesis 17:7) Not that the Covenant is inherited along bloodlines — that's where Judaism and Christianity part company. The baptism of infants is an eloquent testimony to the fact that God always makes the first move, just as he did with Abraham and Sarah. Before an infant is even aware of anything — of God or sacraments or faith or even church pot-lucks and bazaars — before all of that, God makes his move. The Covenant promise is already there, reaching out, surrounding us, enfolding us, marking us with the seal of the Holy Spirit. As a beloved hymn extols:

Now thank we all our God
with heart and hands and voices,
who wondrous things hath done,
in whom this world rejoices;
who, from our mother's arms
hath blessed us on our way
with countless gifts of love,
and still is ours today.

(M. Rinckart, 1636)

In the Covenant, God makes the first move. Baptism is the sign that we have been elected by God to enter into the Covenant. It is first and foremost a sacrament of God's grace. However, it does require a response.

Part C: The Response of Faith

Genesis 17:15-17 — And God said to Abraham, "As for Sarai your wife, you shall not call her name Sarai, but Sarah shall be her name. I will bless her, and moreover I will give you a son by her; I will bless her, and she shall be a mother of nations; kings of peoples shall come from her." Then Abraham fell on his face and laughed, and said to himself, "Shall a child be born to a man who is a hundred years old? Shall Sarah, who is ninety years old, bear a child?"

Is this the same Abraham, the epitome of faith, of whom Saint Paul wrote "no distrust made him waver concerning the promise of God, but he grew strong in his faith as he gave glory to God, fully convinced that God was able to do what he had promised"? (Romans 4:20-21)

Indeed, the very same. The laughter of Abraham is not the same kind of involuntary laughter that is so contagious in the pew where the high schoolers are seated. No, this laughter is different. It is a disbelieving, mocking, irreverent, and skeptical laughter. "HA! God, you're putting me on! Don't be ridiculous. You can't possibly give me a child through Sarah. We're barren. Haven't you heard?"

It's healthy for those of us in the twentieth century to see Abraham laughing. In that one image, the 4,000 years that stand between us are swept aside. The modern mind didn't invent religious doubt after all. It's been there all along. Here is one who, like us, also struggled to believe against hope. Abraham was hardly the last person to laugh at God.

- That job that is so miserable, that boss that you just can't stand? God can transform all that. HA!
- That marriage that's falling apart at the seams. It's not too late to let God patch that up. HA!
- That parent who is constantly on your case. You can accept that person as a human being, with intentions just as good as yours. God will help you do it. HA!

Father Abraham's laughter is that very same raucous guffaw that filters down into all sorts of places in our lives. Why, it is as thick as the air we breathe:

- Here we are on this spinning orb that is nowhere on a galactic map, and we're supposed to believe in God, and a *personal* God at that? *(smile)*
- Look at all the religions that there are in the world. How can Christianity claim to be exclusive? *(chortle)*
- There is so much suffering in the world today, so much injustice and poverty. How can there be a God when so many are in anguish? *(smirk)*
- You talk about a righteous God. Does the name Auschwitz ring a bell?
- God is our Protector, right. But it's also nice to have a few nuclear weapons to back Him up. *(snicker)*

You see, Abraham's laughter echoes down through the ages, right into the present-day. How hard, how desperately hard, it is to believe in God's promises! But is that really why

Abraham laughed, because he had an *intellectual* problem with faith in God? The Bible suggests that Abraham's problem was deeper than that. Fasten your seat belts for this one:

Genesis 17:18 — And Abraham said to God, "O that Ishmael might live in thy sight!"

There's the problem: Ishmael. Ishmael stands for a *spiritual* problem. Abraham wants to hang on to *his* world, what *he* knows, what *he* can control. He wants to avoid the deep and unsettling claim that God is making upon his life. "I'm happy here," he says. "Things are stable. I'm so much more comfortable in a closed universe. No surprises, please. Why don't you just give the promise to Ishmael?"

"No way," says God. "I am going to do this *my* way. Let go of Ishmael. The child of promise is Isaac."

Genesis 17:19 — Sarah your wife shall bear you a son, and you shall call his name Isaac (that is, "he laughs"). I will establish my covenant with him as an everlasting covenant for his descendants after him."

Is anything impossible for God? That is the question that Abraham faced. And that is the question that every person must face, sooner or later. Either you can play it safe with Ishmael, and say "Yes, there really are some things that are too hard for God; I'll stick with my own devices, thank you;" or you can embrace Isaac, the child of promise, the one who laughs, as a way of saying: "With God, all things are possible. Take my life and do with it what you will, Lord."

It's ultimately a question of whether you wish to go through life laughing *at* God or *with* God.

Lent 3

The Precepts of the Lord

Sign: Ten Commandments

Scripture:
*Exodus 20:1-17;
Psalm 18 [19]:7-14
1 Corinthians 1:22-25
John 2:13-22

The Covenant is a Covenant of Law. WHOA! Isn't the *Christian* Covenant a covenant of grace, as opposed to works? Doesn't Saint Paul complain that the Law, the "dispensation of death," kills, while only the Spirit gives life? (2 Corinthians 3:6-7)

"Law" has often gotten bad press among Christians. While not arguing for the kind of legalism that rightly offended Jesus and very nearly made a neurotic out of Saint Paul, there are some positive features of God's Law.

1. Martin Luther, who waged a famous quarrel with the Law, acknowledged that there was at least one positive purpose of Law: it condemns us and throws us upon God's mercy.[12]

How is God's Law so encountered? Answer: through what theologians refer to as Natural Law. Natural Law is the way in which each person, through reflection about life, society, and sexuality, is naturally led to an inner moral code, such as we have in the Ten Commandments. The Ten Commandments make sense. They are a reasonable system of ethics for the human race. They are Natural Law, and therefore binding upon all.[13]

But if God's Law is so reasonable, then why do we need

an actual Ten Commandments? In other words, if each person knows inwardly in his or her own conscience, what is basically right and wrong, why then are the Ten Commandments necessary?

The thirteenth-century theologian Thomas Aquinas asked this question. He concluded that an external code of ethics is needed because people are all too often inwardly led astray by passion and ignorance. For this reason, God has provided an objective revelation of Natural Law, as embodied in the Ten Commandments. They tell us what we could figure out on our own, naturally, were it not for our ignorance and passion.

Ignorance about God's law needs no comment. I will comment on passion because I see that a few heads are beginning to nod. Passion refers to the overriding of morality by emotion. Somehow, passion is supposed to make a violation of God's law a little more understandable.

For example, it is to the advantage of someone on trial for the defense counsel to convince the jury that while the crime was indeed committed, it was a crime of passion, and not premeditated. That is supposed to make it understandable, perhaps even forgivable.

Or, this example: the conscience of persons caught in extramarital affairs are eased somewhat by the passion that they feel for each other. They do not consider themselves adulterers (which is what they are) because their emotions "got carried away."

Of course, nothing can match the passion with which every one of us routinely alters the truth in order to cast ourselves in the best light possible.

Such examples illustrate the necessity for an objective, externalized summary of Natural Law, as we have in the Ten Commandments. God knows that internalized natural law can become subjective — meaning that while it is based upon reason, one can never be sure that reason is always present.

The Ten Commandments, as an expression of Natural Law, are *objective*. That's why God has given the them to us. God knows all too well that the human conscience is infinitely capable of all kinds of rationalizing when it comes to questions of right and wrong — particularly when self-interest is involved. God knows that, given half a chance, the human conscience can wiggle out of anything.

But God's Law, expressed in an external, objective code, is always there, always the same. No matter what goes on in the human family, the Law remains, there, over all of us. It is not swayed by our excuses and justifications, nor is it sympathetic to what we claim are "mitigating circumstances." God's Law has a convicting purpose. It helps us positively to identify sin. It teaches us the sure knowledge of right and wrong.

The Laws of God (just like the laws of nature) remain operative, in effect for everyone, all the time. They are never suspended — not during war, not during a night out on the town, not during a parish council meeting, not even when we, for a change, hold our tongues. God's standard is always there — an objective statement of principle, over and apart from us. It is, therefore, more trustworthy, for it judges us no matter how ingenious our consciences are in excusing themselves from responsibility.

God's Law sets the standards for the social contract, and condemns our failures to meet those standards. The first purpose of God's Law is a spiritual one: to convict. The Law makes us realize that we cannot fulfill God's demands, and causes us, as Luther wrote, to throw ourselves upon his mercy.[14]

2. God's Law also has a *civil purpose*.[15] The legal codes of Western civilizations are based upon Roman law and the Ten Commandments. God's Law establishes a social contract. The state is entrusted as God's agent to preserve order, to uphold the law, and to punish transgressors as God's arm of justice. This is a God-given right and duty of those who

govern. That is why we pray for our rulers, who are given the difficult task of preserving order and peace and thwarting anarchy.

Granted, there are inherent tensions here, capital punishment being one. The state, in its desire to uphold the commandment "Thou shalt not kill," may itself violate it in sentencing someone to death. There are some persuasive arguments against capital punishment:

a. It is not a proven deterrent to others.

b. As a means of simply disposing of society's problems, it is absolutely immoral.

c. As an "eye-for-an-eye, tooth-for-a-tooth" kind of ethic, it is vindictive and unbecoming of a civilized order.

d. As a form of justice, it is unfairly apportioned to poor and black persons, who, because they cannot afford the best legal counsel, may lose their lives.

From the Christian perspective, there is an additional argument against capital punishment: it is a denial of God's redemptive power. No matter how confused, or dangerous, or despicable is the convict on Death Row, *society* needs to believe that God can still redeem, that God can still forgive, that God can still rehabilitate and restore, and that God upholds the sanctity of life.

Society desperately needs that vision *for itself!* We may not have a clue as to how a desperate criminal can be redeemed. We may give up on that person and sentence him to death, cutting him off from the land of the living. *But God doesn't!* As humans, we need to believe that there is always hope — for each of us has more in common with the condemned man than we dare to admit!

So much for the second purpose of the Law, to restrain the evildoer. The excursus on capital punishment was included at no extra charge.

3. The third purpose of God's Law is what John Calvin

called the *teaching purpose*. The Law guides the Christian in the paths of faithful obedience. Calvin wrote that even the believing Christian has need of the Law — not to earn God's grace, which cannot be earned, but rather to respond in gratefulness to God's grace.[16]

The psalm for today expresses this as well:

The law of the Lord is perfect,
*   reviving the soul;*
the testimony of the Lord is sure,
*   making wise the simple;*
The precepts of the Lord are right,
*   rejoicing the heart;*
the commandment of the Lord is pure,
*   enlightening the eyes;*
The fear of the Lord is clean,
*   enduring forever;*
the ordinances of the Lord are true,
*   and righteous altogether.*
More to be desired are they than gold,
*   even much fine gold;*
sweeter also than honey
*   and drippings of the honeycomb.*
Moreover by them is thy servant warned;
*   in keeping them there is great reward.*

Psalm 18 (19):7-11

Many preachers have extolled grace at the expense of Law. This sermon has followed a different course. It has pointed out Law's positive role in the life of faith and the ordering of society. To review: 1. The Law has a *convicting purpose:* it condemns us and drives us to throw ourselves upon God's mercy. 2. It has a *civic purpose:* it is the basis for the social contract and gives to those who govern a divine mandate to preserve peace and order, based upon justice. 3. And, the Law has a *teaching purpose:* it helps the Christian to live a life of faithful obedience.

The Covenant is a Covenant of Law, yes. But there is more! Tune in again next week to find out in what sense *grace* abrogates the *Law,* how the foolishness of God is wiser than men. (1 Corinthians 1:25)

Lent 4

Good News for Exiles

Sign: Hebrews' restoration

Scripture:
*2 Chronicles 36:14-23
*Psalm 136 [137]:1-6
Ephesians 2:4-10
Saint John 3:14-21

God's Covenant is a Gospel Covenant.

You've heard those words before. But what do they mean? We will approach this through the back door.

There are certain things in life that you can only understand by way of contrast. You cannot know what spring is, until you've experienced a tough winter. You don't really appreciate a Porsche until you've spent five hours in a Maverick. You cannot revel in community until you've languished in loneliness.

That's how it is with Gospel. You cannot know what Gospel is unless you understand what Law is. For those of you who missed church last week, you're in luck. Today's Old Testament lesson shows us the contrast between Law and Gospel.

At the close of the second Book of the Chronicles (or Annals), we find the Hebrew people living in exile, in Babylon (which is in modern-day Iraq). The Babylonians were among the most ruthless and hated of the ancient empire-builders. Their armies pursued a scorched-earth policy, devastating cities such as Jerusalem (597/98 B.C.). After reducing their enemies' cities to rubble, they would then deport any survivors to Babylon. Under the watchful eye of the central authorities, they settled them there in colonies.

Do you think modern-day New York City is cosmopolitan? It doesn't begin to compare with ancient Babylon, where innumerable peoples lived in a vast megalopolis. The Hebrews were there, along with all the others. They, too, were forced to worship the official gods of the Babylonian state religion. But it fell to Israel's unique calling as a Covenant community to see in this bitter turn of events the hand of God, to interpret their fate as God's punishment for being unfaithful to God's laws:

> 2 Chronicles 36:15-16 — The Lord, the God of their fathers, sent persistently to them by his messengers, because he had compassion on his people and on his dwelling place; but they kept mocking the messengers of God, despising his words, and scoffing at his prophets, till the wrath of the Lord rose against his people, till there was no remedy.

The moral here: There's a price to be paid when you tangle with God's Law. It was Babylon who rang the death knell on Judah. Wicked Babylon, detested Babylon became an instrument of God's Law. God used Babylon to crack down on Judah. When Judah was destroyed by Babylon's advancing armies, when the Hebrews were hauled off by them into exile, the righteous God simply turned and looked the other way.

What's it like to be an exile? Exile means: having no home; living in a strange place where the food, the language, the weather, the politics are all unfamiliar — and uncomfortable.

For Jews in Babylon, exile meant all of that and more. It also meant being cut off from their religious life, which had been centered in the Temple at Jerusalem, now a pile of rubble. They were cut off from God. They couldn't worship, they couldn't pray, spiritually they couldn't live.

"How shall we sing the Lord's song in a foreign land?" they cried in a psalm written during this period. If I forget

Jerusalem, my home, may my tongue cleave to the roof of my mouth. In utter dejection, they hung up their lyres, and by the waters of Babylon, they sat and wept. (Psalm 136 [137])
They wept because:

- what had happened to them was so terrible;
- God had abandoned them, so they thought;
- they had no hope for their future;
- they were being ridiculed and degraded;
- they no longer believed in themselves as a people;
- they faced the awful truth about themselves: they had disobeyed God's Law;
- they learned the hard way about the darker side of God's Covenant: that a righteous God punishes those who are not obedient.

That's why the Hebrews wept. And while, pray God, we may never be deported into exile, we know what it's like to weep — if not outwardly, then inwardly.

That's where the story of the Jews connects with our lives today. The Jews' exile is a microcosm: it stands for the universal human experience of exile, with which all of God's people can identify. We recognize in their tears our own tears, our own pain.

In other words, you don't need to go off to a Babylon to be an exile. You can be an exile right at home, in your own head, right in your own body, right in your own heart. It means not knowing who you are. It means being alienated from God:

The Jews' experience of exile helps us to identify our own experience of exile:

- when you tangle with God's law, you're an exile;
- when you despair over fulfilling the demand of God's Law, you're an exile;
- when you hit rock bottom low and are in utter confusion, you're an exile;
- when you can say with the psalmist:

For I know my transgressions, and my sin is ever before me. Against thee, thee only, have I sinned, and done that which is evil in thy sight, so that thou art justified in thy sentence and blameless in thy judgment.

Psalm 50 (51):3-4

You're an exile.

- When you've sinned against God's people and alienated yourself from the church, you're an exile.
- When you've hurt your spouse or child or become estranged from friends and relatives, you're an exile.
- When you feel your life going under, down into the Pit, you're an exile.

You don't have to go off to a Babylon to be an exile. You can be one right at home: right in your own head; right in your own body; right in your own heart.

Exile is the experience of all who tangle with God's Law. The demand of God's Law condemns us to exile — an experience that is seering, painful, debilitating, and crushing — because we know just how far away from God we are.

The church, in its wisdom, knows that this can happen in the life of the Christian, any Christian. That's what this season is all about. Lent is designed for exiles. It's a time to deal with those things that cut us off from life, that separate us from the Land of the Living, that choke off our prayer life, that poison our spirituality, that stand between us and God. Lent is for exiles — for Christians in their "dark night of the soul," whenever it may come, whenever it may come again.

Lent is for those in Babylon.

You will recall that this sermon was supposed to be on Gospel. So far, all we've talked about is Law, and its consequences: exile. Well, that's the contrast you need to begin to understand Gospel.

The Good News is that when you find yourself in exile, *God makes ready His move.* Just as surely as Babylon was for the Hebrews God's instrument of Law, the Edict of Cyrus was God's instrument of grace.

The Persians under Cyrus pursued a much more enlightened policy than that of the Babylonians. The Persians built their more advanced empire on the progressive principle of pluralism. They were willing to respect, instead of stifle, the differences of the various subjugated peoples. A wise policy! Their empire lasted some two hundred years, until Alexander the Great assembled an even greater one.

Significantly, the Edict of Cyrus, which authorized the Jews' return to the Holy Land and the reconstruction of their Temple, came quite suddenly and unexpectedly. Out of the blue, it caught everyone by surprise. The Hebrews had surely done nothing to deserve it, nor expect it. But there it was! And, most amazing of all, the arm of God's grace was Cyrus, *an unbeliever!* You mean God can work through other peoples as well?

That's Gospel! Gospel means that God totally surprises you — it means that God accepts you despite your unacceptability. As Saint Paul says, "By grace you have been saved through faith; and this is not your own doing, it is the *gift* of God." (Ephesians 2:8) Gospel: you can't earn it, expect it, or predict it. Sometimes, when it comes, you don't even recognize it for what it is: Gospel.

We hinted at this last week when we looked at the Ten Commandments, the heart of the Mosaic Law, and pointed out some ways in which even the Law contains Gospel. Is it not also a gift of God's grace? You see, the harder you look, the thinner the line between Law and Gospel becomes. Take, for example, Jesus' Sermon on the Mount. Is that Law, or Gospel? Do we find Law in the Old Testament and Gosple in the New Testament? Hardly. Law and Gospel are scattered throughout the books of both the Old and the New Testaments. How about the Hebrews' exile in Babylon? Law, right? But don't forget that during that difficult period, the synagogue developed, the institution that would enable the Jewish faith to survive in the millennia ahead. You see how God is always looking ahead? Even exile in Babylon, as bitter as that experience was, contained a mixture of Law and grace.

Every age, every experience in life, is both a time of Law, and a time of Gospel. Law and Gospel are but two sides of the same coin:

The Law shows us sin	*The Gospel shows us grace;*
The Law reveals the disease	*The Gospel gives us the cure;*
The Law is a demand	*The Gospel is a gift;*
The Law reveals a God who is a righteous judge	*The Gospel reveals the same God, but as one who is a compassionate Savior.*

No wonder Luther concluded that the distinction between Law and Gospel "contains the sum of all Christian doctrine"!

God's Covenant is a Covenant of LAW.
God's Covenant is a Covenant of GRACE.

They are but two sides of the same coin. That makes God's Covenant a lot like marriage. Every marriage has its law side. There are rules, agreements, and expectations, to be sure. But in marriage, there are inevitably infractions of the rules, misunderstandings about agreements, and disappointments over failed expectations. When such things happen, the temptation is to apply the Law. But, if the marriage is to survive, you can't hold these things against the other person, which is what law does. Such things need to be overlooked and forgiven. That's the Gospel side of marriage, a side that is based upon a profound sense of the other person as *gift* — God's gift.

Next week, we will see how the partners in God's marriage Covenant "fell in love all over again," and how that love is nourished by Christ, our great high priest.

Lent 5

Written Upon Their Hearts

Sign: The indwelling of the Holy Spirit

Scripture:
*Jeremiah 31:31-34
Psalm 50 [51]:10-17
*Hebrews 5:7-10
Saint John 12:20-33

"Behold, the days are coming," says the Lord, "when I will make a new covenant with the house of Israel and the house of Judah . . . I will put my law within them, and I will write it upon their hearts; and I will be their God, and they shall be my people."

Jeremiah 31:31, 33b

One of the first words an infant learns is the word *no.* Holding to the side of the glass-top coffee table, the baby lunges for the crystal vase upon it. "No," cries the mother. "No, *no!"*

The child is confused, startled, and hurt. She only wishes to examine this fascinating object — first by feeling it, then by tasting it. A slap on her wrists reinforces the verbal message. Some things in life are forbidden — and, apparently, from the child's perspective, for rather arbitrary reasons.

At our next visit, we see the same child at age three. Much more mobile, her verbal and intellectual skills noticeably advance with each passing day. The repertoire of rules is now considerably expanded. No Crayola drawing on the wall; no playing with food at the table; no sitting on the dog; no going outside without mother or father.

While the structure of prohibitions is still arbitrary from

the child's perspective, some are now beginning to make more sense — such as the one against playing in the street. The child understands that this rule is in her own self-interest. Very possibly, therefore, there may be some design to the structure of rules and limitations being imposed on her.

· The child also now has a clear sense of what might happen if the rules are broken — for each rule that has been established has been tested — to see if it really *is* a rule. The child actively explores the outer limits of the parents' authority, which are determined by punishment or the threat of punishment.

We leave those years of discovery, frustration, and occasional tantrums, and look briefly at the six-year-old child — dutifully trudging off to school, bringing home a picture with a "plus" on it. Proudly, she presents it to her parents for their approval. The six-year-old has come to a certain truce with the rules of the household. Now they are not so much questioned, as simply obeyed. More importantly, obedience to the rules is connected to the belief that somehow the parents' love and acceptance go along with that. Six-year-olds are pleasers. They want to be good children — so that their parents will affirm and love them, so they think.

It is this myth that the child *earns* the parents' love through obedience that helps to explain what we find at age thirteen. Here is a rebellious teenager, who aggressively challenges this very link between obedience and parents' acceptance. Every new development brings a challenge to authority. "What do you mean, I can't do that? Who says? Why not?"

There is a sharply defiant tone in her voice — a challenge to her parents to prove that she is not grown up. She begins to smoke. She spends hours on the phone with her friend, at whose house she will often stay over without first asking her parents' permission. She attends other churches for awhile and then drops out of church entirely. She wastes hours of her time watching TV, is content with "C"s, and fawns over teen idols.

The parents stand by patiently, reading articles on adolescence and hoping for time to bring some maturity to their daughter. Their attempts at communication are inevitably cut off by this "child in an adult's body," who stomps out of the room with the angry accusation, "You don't love me!"

Tensions between parents and child inevitably move toward a climax of some kind, and it is hoped, a breakthrough. It is impossible to predict what sequence of events might lead such individuals to that final confrontation — when the love and patience of parents are put to their most severe test. When this happens, all the chips are suddenly on the table. It usually catches parents quite by surprise. Suddenly, they are in the battle of their lives, and the stakes are high. They may lose (or re-gain) their daughter.

In the case of the girl we have followed from infancy, the crisis point comes in her eighteenth year, during the summer following her high school graduation. Despite her lackluster GPA, her parents have managed to convince her to give college a try, and have enrolled her in a small, church-related, liberal arts school. Somehow, it is hoped, she will find herself there and do some growing up under the watchful eye of whomever is willing to assume an *in loco parentis* role.

However, parents sometimes have a way of hoping beyond reason. This realization comes sickeningly home to the mother when, late one August evening, her daughter asks to speak with her alone in her room. The mother enters to find a very distraught daughter, nervously fumbling for her lighter, who blurts out the news: "Mom, I'm pregnant."

The mother is shocked, although not surprised. The daughter had been taking advantage of her recently-relaxed curfew.

The daughter and mother begin to talk — for the first time in a long while. It is painful at first, but soon they begin to share the anguish of her situation and the dilemma that she now faces. There is anger and guilt aplenty, of course, as they explore options for the future.

In an off-guarded moment, the mother criticizes her daughter's carelessness and questions the motives and character of the young man in question.

And that's when it happens.

"Mother," the daughter screams, "you have never liked my friends, and have always blamed me for anything that goes wrong. If anybody's to blame for this," she fumes with tears welling up in her eyes, "it's *you!*"

"Me? Why? What did *I* do to get you pregnant?" the mother shoots back in astonishment.

"You never touched me nor made me feel like I was loved," the daughter charges.

The mother is deeply wounded by this attack. For as far back as she can remember, the daughter has pulled back from her affection, resisting her loving embrace. As her emotions reach the boiling point, she refuses to accept her daughter's reckless accusation:

"Daughter, what on earth are you *saying?* Don't you know how much your father and I love you — no matter what you do?"

The mother bursts into anguished sobs.

"We have tried to do so much for you. We have loved you since before you were even born. We have put up with so much. Do you have any idea how much you have hurt us?"

The daughter has never seen her mother in such an intensely emotional state. She has not ever realized that her own pain was more than matched by her mother's. This "other person," this authority figure against whom she has spent her whole life reacting, this strong person she secretly admires but knows she could never be, is actually very human, very committed to her, and very close to her.

A relationship that has always been primarily legal in character is now on the verge of becoming primarily personal.

If you have some feel for the depth of emotion in this family portrait, you will be able to grasp the perspective of the prophet Jeremiah.

The genius of the Jewish expression of religion is what we call "Covenant." For Israel, Covenant meant radical faith in one sovereign God. The other religions of antiquity had many gods, who competed with each other for various spheres of power. Not so with the Hebrews. There is only one God, said the Jews, and Yahweh is Lord.

Moreover, this God is not withdrawn from world events, but is very much active in them. The Exodus from Egypt was the experience that most impressed itself upon the psyche of the Hebrew people.

This God chose to have a special Covenant relationship with the Hebrews. The Jews were God's elect from among the nations. This was declared at the time of Abraham, and was sealed in the rite of circumcision, a sign of the Covenant.

Because of Israel's special calling as a nation, there were special obligations to God in return. It was Moses who shaped the childhood of Israel. The Ten Commandments became the core of moral expectations in the family of God. The rules were now considerably more involved than when there was a simple *no,* symbolized by the Tree of Knowledge in the Garden of Eden. After Moses, there was an early adolescent explosion of moral and ritual laws that marked the boundaries for Israel. Dutifully, she trudged off to school to master them.

As Israel moved into later adolescence, she developed a love/hate relationship with all these rules and the God who demanded absolute obedience to them. Over several generations, she struggled with them, sometimes obeying them, sometimes ignoring them, sometimes disobeying them. Slowly but surely, she grew more rebellious, angry that God's love should be linked to obedience, probing the perimeters of God's authority, challenging his wisdom and justice, testing his patience.

Consequently, Israel had all kinds of scrapes and bumps. She flirted with other gods. At one point, she sank so low that she was hauled off in chains to Babylon.

It was sometime after this that the prophet Jeremiah enters the scene. Speaking in behalf of God, Jeremiah promises a New Covenant.

(Excursus:) Traditionally Covenant Theology is divided on the question of whether there are two covenants or just one. It's the sort of dispute that earns people doctorates and keeps seminary students occupied.

The Westminster Confession of Faith says that there are two covenants: a covenant of works and a covenant of grace.

> The first covenant made with man was a covenant of works, wherein life was promised to Adam, and in him to his posterity, upon condition of perfect and personal obedience. Man, by his fall, having made himself incapable of life by that covenant, the Lord was pleased to make a second, commonly called the covenant of grace: wherein he freely offered unto sinners life and salvation by Jesus Christ, requiring of them faith in him, that they may be saved, and promising to give unto all those that are ordained unto life, his Holy Spirit, to make them willing and able to believe.[17]

The Confession apears to agree with Jeremiah. That there are two covenants is also supported by many passages of Scripture,[18] and by the structure of the Bible itself, which is divided into an Old and a New Testament (another word for Covenant).

But the Confession makes a fineline theological distinction. There are not, it says, two covenants of grace differing in substance, but one and the same under various dispensations. In theological circles, that's what's known as "fancy footwork."

The new covenant foretold by Jeremiah is not actually "new" as in "different." It is the same covenant, but reconsecrated and re-established by the blood of Christ. The New Covenant, then, is actually a new perception of the one, continuous Covenant.[19] *(End of excursus.)*

Jeremiah says that in this new experience of the Covenant, God will write his law upon human hearts, meaning that the Law will be *internalized*. There will no longer be a need to teach the Law, for each person will possess a changed heart, each person will know the Lord inwardly, and thereby know what the Lord requires as a matter of course.

How can this happen? How can a heart be so changed?

We suggested, in our mother-daughter analogy, that a changed heart can occur through a dramatic confrontation, precipitated by a seering crisis, in which the child comes to see the parent in a new way.

That is exactly what the Gospel of Jesus Christ does. It shows God in a new light. The author of Hebrews paints a vivid picture of Jesus offering up prayers and supplications *with loud cries and tears*. What an *unusual* description of God!

We had always viewed God as a distant, supreme, lawgiver, who laid down the rules and threatened us into obeying them. We had assumed that God loved us according to how well we behaved! Now we see God differently. Instead, we see a compassionate Savior, upon a cross, who feels deeply for our world, who cries in our behalf, who constantly prays for us. Our perception of God has cut through all the stereotypes *to see the person who was there all along.* That's the New Covenant!

O Daughter (of Zion)! Don't you know how much your father and I love you — no matter what you do? We have tried to do so much for you. We have loved you since before you were even born. We have put up with so much. Do you have any idea how much you have hurt us?

> *"Behold, the days are coming," says the Lord, "when I will make a new covenant with the house of Israel and the house of Judah . . . I will put my law within them, and I will write it upon their hearts; and I will be their God, and they shall be my people."*

Palm/Passion Sunday

Have This Mind

Sign: Baptism

Scripture:
Saint Mark 11:1-11
*Isaiah 50:4-9a
Psalm 30:10-17 (RC), 31:9-16 (Protestant)
*Philippians 2:5-11
Saint Mark 14:1—15:47

We Earthlings have our own way of looking at things. Perspective is determined by what lies at our center. Conditioned by values and environment, we see what we want to see. Just how true that is was evident when a NASA scientist briefed the media on Voyager 2's mission to the planet Uranus.

"Uranus," he said, "has many more moons than previously thought — fifteen, not five. Furthermore, they have more radically sculpted surfaces than anything seen to date. The rings of Uranus are also different from what we had expected. There are not only a much larger number of them (instead of nine, upwards on one hundred), but they contain boulders and chunks of material. Most intriguing is the nature of the magnetic field, which wobbles from the axis of the planet, which itself has been tipped."

At this point, a reporter interrupted the scientist with a question: "How do you explain such weird phenomena?"

"What do you mean *weird*," asked the scientist. "From what we are learning, it's possible that *Earth* is the oddball, not the norm. Your question betrays a geocentric perspective."

There was a stunned silence in the room, followed by

a gentle laugh.

Yes, we Earthlings have our own way of looking at things, Palm Sunday is a challenge to try some new filters, to look at life and the cosmos from a different perspective. It dares to suggest that "there are more things in heaven and earth . . . than are dreamt of in your philosophy" (*Hamlet,* Act 1, Scene 5).

Saint Paul writes:

2:5-7 — Have this mind among yourselves, which you have in Christ Jesus, who, though he was in the form of God, did not count equality with God a thing to be grasped, but emptied himself . . .

Is Paul a madman? Anyone educated at the Ivy League schools of the Ancient World would have dismissed this as just so much nonsense. God becoming a human being? The idea is preposterous. God is other-worldly, pure spirit, untainted by this corrupted order. How could God join the human race and still be God?

2:7-8 — . . . but emptied himself, taking the form of a servant, being born in the likeness of men. And being found in human form he humbled himself and became obedient unto death, even death on a cross.

Humbled himself? That's Paul for you. A *Hellenistic* Jew, you know. Every *true* Jew, who has stayed at home, knows that the Messiah will be a political savior, who will restore Israel to her former glory, who will expel the hated Romans and usher in God's Kingdom here on earth, centered, of course, in Jerusalem.

Many who shouted "Hosanna" when Jesus entered Jerusalem were looking for this kind of Messiah. Of course, their "Hosannas" were not to be heard on Friday. A Suffering Servant Messiah did not fit with their perspective. "His Kingdom is not of this world, eh? Then what good is it?"

The Gospel of Christ offended the most basic assumptions of Jew and Greek alike. Saint Paul couldn't have expressed it better:

We preach Christ crucified, a stumbling block to the Jews and folly to the Greeks.

1 Corinthians 1:23

The Gospel is no less abrasive to the geocentric perspectives of today. It is a radical challenge to values and assumptions. To be a Christian is hardly the high road to fame and fortune. Its path is a lowly one of servanthood. There is a cost to being a disciple. You must turn your back on the values of this world.

We have suggested throughout Lent that the Covenant necessitates a response to God's initiative. Those who would walk in the Way of the Cross, those who would share in the triumph of the Cross, must take on the mind of Christ.

This week, throughout the world, many will enter the covenant through the Sacrament of Baptism at Easter. As they confess their faith before the church, they will be asked to turn their backs upon the values and perspectives of this world. In the Renunciations, the candidates will be asked:

1. "Do you renounce Satan and all the spiritual forces of wickedness that rebel against God?" Note that evil is not some vague, impersonal force, but a personal force that actively works against God.

2. "Do you renounce the evil powers of this world which corrupt and destroy the creatures of God?" Implied in this renunciation are those tremendously powerful forces that are hurtful to human society and to God (including racism, militarism, consumerism, sexism, bigotry, and wanton disregard for the environment).

3. Do you renounce all sinful desires that draw you from the love of God?" Evil corrupts the personal life as well, tempting us to give in to hatred, back-biting, jealousy, envy, strife, dissension, lust, self-pity. These are the forces of evil that threaten to undo us from within.

Baptism is the church's prayer that those who enter it will have the mind of Christ, will turn from sin, and will continue to renounce it throughout their lives. That's why renunciations are used even in the Baptism of infants, who are too little to know what evil is. Baptism marks the beginning of the Christian pilgrimage, which consists of spiritual warfare against the powers of evil. It is entrance into the Covenant and the acceptance of responsibilities therein.

Yes, we Earthlings have our own way of looking at things. But so does God. Holy Week invites us to view the cosmos through God's eyes, by putting Christ at the center.

God has highly exalted him and bestowed on him the name which is above every name, that at the name of Jesus every knee should bow, in heaven and on earth and under the earth, and every tongue confess that Jesus Christ is Lord, to the glory of God the Father.

Philippians 2:9-11

Holy or Maundy Thursday

Poured Out for Many

Signs: Passover, Eucharist

Scripture:
*Exodus 24:3-8
Psalm 115 [116]:12-19
1 Corinthians 10:16-17
Saint Mark 14:12-16

And Moses took the blood and threw it upon the people, and said, "Behold the blood of the covenant which the LORD has made with you in accordance with these words."

Exodus 24:8

The symbol of blood is both an attraction and a revulsion to Christian piety. For some, it is a rich expression of religious feeling. The hymnwriter says: "There is a fountain filled with blood, drawn from Immanuel's veins; And sinners plunged beneath that flood Lose all their guilty stains." (W. Cowper, 1779)

However, others feel that the Christian religion should rise above such primal imagery. Christianity, they say, is a mature, spiritual religion. It is regressive to mix in such materialistic imagery as blood. This may even translate into feelings of ambivalence about taking Holy Communion, because of its reference to Christ's blood poured out for many.

The ancient Hebrews who gathered under Moses at Mount Sinai to seal their covenant in blood, may not have understood the Rh factor or the mysteries of hemoglobin. But they *did* understand that blood stood for life. Quite naturally, their religious instincts guided them to the conclusion that blood was sacred, for it was life. Everything that touches life is in close contact with God, who is the origin of all life.

For the Hebrews, this understanding of blood brought three immediate consequences:

a. The first was ethical. Murder is a violation of God's Law. To spill another person's blood is to deprive God of God's own power over life and death. Therefore, it is wrong.

b. The second consequence was a ritual one. Blood is not to be consumed. Blood, like life, belongs only to God and is not to be eaten. Kosher food laws, in which a rabbi verifies that food has been properly bled before it is blessed and consumed, have their origin here.

c. The third consequence was liturgical. Because blood is linked to life and therefore to God, it may appropriately be used in acts of worship, such as the covenant-making at Mount Sinai.

To the Hebrew people gathered there, Moses reads God's Word, detailing God's expectations of them. They solemnly swear to do as God wants. Then Moses seals the covenant between the Hebrews and God in blood, the blood of an innocent victim. Half of the blood he throws upon the altar (symbol for God's presence): half of the blood he throws on the people.

With blood, the Lord and the Hebrews are bound together in an indissoluble covenant. Yahweh will always be her God. Israel will always belong to THE LORD.

The Covenant with Israel, which Moses seals in blood, is a pre-figuration of the New Covenant in Christ. One of the great themes of Covenant Theology is the way in which the Old Covenant is understood to foreshadow the New:

Pre-Figuration	Fulfillment
Noah's Flood	Baptism
The faith of Abraham and Sarah	The faith of the church and the individual Christian

Pre-Figuration	Fulfillment
Circumcision	Baptism
The Law, given on Mount Sinai	The New Law, given in a sermon atop a mount
The exile in Babylon and restoration	The sinner's exile and restoration into the new Jerusalem, the church
The Passover	The Eucharist

The New Covenant reveals what was only dimly perceived in the Old. The New Covenant perfects and fulfills that which was begun in the Old. The New Israel takes the religious ideas of the Old Israel and re-wires them completely, transforming their meaning.

The New Testament story of the suffering and death of Christ does exactly that with the symbol of blood. This was not a quantum leap forward in religious development. For centuries, people had begun to question the use of blood in religious rituals. The Greeks, of course, had long thought that such things were quite beneath them. Too materialistic! Even some Jewish prophets agreed. They began to make provocative statements such as "I desire steadfast love and not sacrifice, the knowledge of God, rather than burnt offerings." (Hosea 6:6) Many Jews were content simply to pour out drops of wine on the table at Passover time, in remembrance of the blood shed in the Exodus.

By the time of Jesus, sacrifices and blood rituals were clearly on the wane. There were still plenty of people around who believed in them. But by Jesus' time, the synagogue, not the Temple, was the backbone of Jewish religious life. Enough Jews had "outgrown" the concept of sacrifice, making it only a matter of time. The refinement of religious ideas is a difficult trend to reverse.

If blood was on the way out in liturgy by the time of Jesus, why do we hear so much about it in the New Testament? The answer is a simple one: God moves when humankind is ready! Covenant Theology affirms a God who is actively involved in the human race and its religious development. God grows with us, so to speak.

If you're looking for a religion that never changes, you've picked the wrong one. The Christian faith is constantly evolving, constantly growing in its perception of God's Kingdom. Each generation adds some new insight, some new perception.

The early church was on the cutting edge in its re-working of the concept of blood in religion. The New Testament boldly proclaims that the blood sacrifices of the Temple are now obsolete. The sacrifices of Jesus' blood upon the cross is the final, perfect sacrifice. Any further sacrifices are unnecessary, for Jesus' blood is sufficient to cover the sins of all, forever.

When early Christians use the word "sacrifice," they aren't talking anymore about animals in the Temple at Jerusalem. Instead, they refer to Christ's sacrifice on Calvary. When they describe their early Eucharists as a sacrifice, what they mean is that in the Eucharist the church offers a sacrifice of praise and thanksgiving. Most significantly, Christians begin to talk of *themselves* as sacrifices, about witnessing to their faith by being "living sacrifices, holy and acceptable to God." (Romans 12:1)[20]

The early Christians took the Hebrew ideas about blood and sacrifice and totally revolutionized them. Jesus is proclaimed as *the* innocent victim whose blood is shed for many. His is the sacrifice that ends all sacrifices. The blood that seals this New Covenant is his own blood. And those who drink from this cup, at the Lord's Table, share in this Covenant.

That's what blood means in Christian worship today. And if you still don't feel all that comfortable with it, let me ask you this question: What makes you think that you are *supposed* to feel comfortable with it? Just because you live in a generation that knows much about platelets and antigens, is blood any *less* sacred? Is it any less mysterious as a sign for life itself? I don't think so.

Maybe the problem is not how you feel about blood. Maybe the problem is how you feel about *ritual* and encountering God through it.

The great temptation with ritual is to try to *domesticate* it; to *bring it under control;* to *understand* everything that is going on. But this attitude toward worship violates the most basic terms of the Covenant. The Covenant is a relationship between unequals, one of whom just happens to be Yahweh, the Lord God Almighty, the Holy One, who is shrouded in mystery, who will not let us set foot on Mount Sinai, lest we see him and die.

We have mentioned how the Old Covenant pre-figures the New Covenant. This view of the Covenant tends to exaggerate the differences between Old and New. It portrays the Israelites as "groping in the darkness," in contrast to the Christians who walk as "children of the light."

There is some legitimacy to that. When the Hebrews were being sprinkled with blood, they had no idea that twelve centuries later, Christ would shed his blood on a cross as a fulfillment of what they had started. They hadn't a clue about that!

Possibly, our participation in the Lord's Supper pre-figures something that we can only now dimly perceive — like the wedding feast of the Lamb perhaps? Maybe when we drink Christ's blood of the New Covenant, we are looking through a glass darkly, drawn into a great Mystery that far exceeds our perceptual abilities.

I would go even further and suggest that the communion language about blood is *intended* to throw you off a bit. An elder once complained to a pastor about the use of a common loaf and cup in communion. "It's so messy," she said, "it looks so *untidy.*" The minister thought for a moment and replied: "Perchance, does that remind you of anything?"

Christ's blood of the New Covenant which is poured out for many is the reason why all of us are here tonight. What God had to do to gather us into the Covenant was not at all tidy, not at all un-messy, and we don't need to go into the reasons behind that!

But God did it! God did what needed to be done, praised be he! And next year, may be bring us to Jerusalem!

Good Friday

Christ Our High Priest

Sign: The Cross of Christ

Scripture:
*Isaiah 52:13—53:12
Psalm 21 [22]:1-18
Hebrews 4:14-16, 5:7-9
Saint John 18:1—19:42

Good Friday is a day of conversion. It is a day that focuses on the stark symbol of the cross, upon which our Lord sealed the New Covenant in the shedding of his blood.

Just what was accomplished on the cross? The answer to that question is summarized in one word: Atonement. Atonement means a reconciliation of two parties. You can remember this by breaking down the word by syllables: at-one-ment. The sacrifice of Jesus on the cross achieves an at-one-ment of humankind with God.

How did this happen? Down through the years, there have been three main interpretations of the Atonement, three theories about Christ's saving work on the cross.[21]

Those who are familiar with SLR cameras know that the choice of the lens makes all the difference in the world. During this sermon, we are going to look at the cross through three different lenses.

A. Christus Victor: The Classic Idea

The first lens you will need is a 28mm wide angle one. With it, we will be able to stand at the foot of the cross and still see a great deal. Through this lens, we focus on the fact that the work of Christ on the cross is something that God himself does. The cross is God's own saving work.

God has to do this because humankind, through the Fall, had become totally enslaved to sin, the law, death, and the devil. This enslavement is so complete that only God can step forward to liberate humankind. And liberate he does!

According to this perspective, the cross is the occasion for a colossal showdown between the forces of good and evil. As we stand and gaze up at the head of the cross we see, over and above it, spiritual forces engaged in combat. The spiritual future of the whole world hangs in the balance.

But God dramatically triumphs — because God has offered his only Son as a ransom, paid to the Devil. The Devil accepts this ransom and frees the human race, restoring mankind to its rightful owner.

The important thing here is that God takes the initiative: Divine love triumphs over the powers of evil; God himself personally establishes a new covenant relationship with mankind. God himself pays a ransom to the Devil.

B. Latin Theory of Satisfaction (Anselm)

Now bring the camera down, remove the wide angle lens, and put on a standard 50mm lens. Step back from the cross to the front pew and look through the viewfinder.

What do we see from this perspective? We see that the disobedience of mankind is a great affront to God's honor. God is so offended by humanity's sin that we must offer something to satisfy God.

Here is the crux of the problem. What can sinful humanity possibly offer to satisfy God's offended honor. Absolutely nothing. No living creature, in this fallen order, is able to satisfy God's justice, and merit God's favor. Humankind needs to offer something to God, but humankind has nothing that will be acceptable.

For this reason, God himself must offer satisfaction to God! However, this offering must come from humankind, since it is in behalf of humankind.

The solution to this dilemma is for God to become human, so that in the person of Christ, humankind can pay the satisfaction that God's justice requires. Because Christ's offering is sinless, it is more than sufficient. Christ takes upon himself the punishment due to all, thereby satisfying God's just demands.

Standing at the foot of the cross, we saw God moving toward humankind. Standing further back, we now see a reverse movement: humankind, through the human nature of Christ, moving toward God.

C. Moral Influence Theory (Abelard [1079-1142])

Now put on a third lens — a 200mm telephoto lens. You will need to take this picture of the cross from the balcony.

From this distant perspective, the details of the cross are less apparent. Nonetheless, we are easily able to get the entire cross in our field of vision.

As we ponder the cross from this perspective, we note that it has a strange power over us. It captures our imaginations and hearts, prompting changes within us. We are moved by this "old rugged cross," so moved, in fact, that we resolve to live better lives, to follow the perfect example of the Ideal Man, Jesus Christ.

No longer are we afraid of God and God's justice, for the Cross shows us that God loves us, that God would even go so far as to sacrifice his own Son for us. What a powerful demonstration of God's love! Our hearts are utterly transformed by this event. Our lives are drawn closer to God! We join with others and sing of this change in our lives: "When I survey the wondrous cross on which the Prince of Glory died, My richest gain I count but loss, and pour contempt on all my pride."

From our distant vantage point, the cross has a tremendous moral influence on the human race, inspiring it to move closer to God.

We have now taken our three photos, and will send off

the film to await the developing.

Perhaps you are wondering at this point how it is that the church could have three different explanations on something so central to the Christian faith as Christ's saving work upon the Cross. Shouldn't there be just one teaching on the Atonement? Which one, you ask, is the right one?

This is why we chose the analogy of photography. No picture accurately portrays its subject. A photo is not a picture of reality, but only a perspective on reality. The use of different lenses provides differing perspectives on the subject.

Well then, what does the Bible say about the Atonement? Interestingly, the lessons for Good Friday include all three perspectives, each influenced by a different lens.

In his moving poetry about the Suffering Servant who will redeem Israel, the prophet, Isaiah writes.

Behold, my servant shall prosper,
  he shall be exalted and lifted up,
  and shall be very high.
As many were astonished at him —
  his appearance was so marred, beyond
    human semblance,
  and his form beyond that of the sons of men —
So shall he startle many nations;
  kings shall shut their mouths because of him;
for that which has not been told them
  they shall see,
and that which they have not heard
  they shall understand.

                                        Isaiah 52:13-15

That sounds like what we saw through our telephoto lens from a distance. The human race is shamed by the cross. Overcome by its moral appeal, we are inspired to move closer to God.

But a few verses away, we read:

Surely he has borne our griefs
and carried our sorrows;
yet we esteemed him stricken,
smitten by God, and afflicted.
But he was wounded for our transgressions,
he was bruised for our iniquities;
upon him was the chastisement that made us whole,
and with his stripes we are healed.
All we like sheep have gone astray;
we have turned every one to his own way:
and the Lord has laid on him
the iniquity of us all.

Isaiah 53:4-6

The Suffering Servant satisfies God's offended honor, by offering himself as a sacrifice. Now that sounds like what we saw through our standard 50mm lens.

In the Gospel reading from Saint John, we read these words:

My kingship is not of this world; if my kingship were of this world, my servants would fight, that I might not be handed over to the Jews; but my kingship is not from the world.

John 18:36

Now that sounds rather like the view that we got while at the foot of the cross, through our wide-angle lens. The cross signifies a spiritual battle, carried on in our behalf by God in Christ, whose kingdom is not of this world.

The fact is that all three viewpoints about Christ's saving work on the Cross are supported by Scripture. All three, despite their contradictions, contain truth. All three are also necessary, to correct each other and to remind us that the Atonement is essentially a mystery, that no one theory can exhaust its meaning.

When your pictures of the Cross are developed, there will probably be one that you will want to enlarge, mount, and hang on your wall.

I should think that you will want to consider the one that takes very seriously the problem of evil in the world, that sees evil as something so involved that God's intervention is necessary, for humankind is not able to extricate itself without help. I think that you will want to consider the picture of the Cross that will enable you to break that power of evil in your life. Finally, you will want one that will be for you a battlesong of triumph!

Maybe you had better get a frame for all three.

Pascha: The Resurrection of Our Lord

The Fashioning of Christians

Signs: The Resurrection of our Lord; baptismal garments; Christians themselves — sacraments of God's love and mercy.

Scripture:
*Ezekiel 36:24-28

My earliest memory of church is a rather traumatic one. My earliest memory is that of being attacked by a fox. That's right, a fox! The year was 1950. We had just moved to Minneapolis where my father had become an associate pastor in a large, urban congregation. Of course, everyone was anxious to meet the new pastor and his family — at that time, two little boys.

This was a fashionable congregation, full of the 50's version of Yuppies. That year, the women of the church were all sporting boas, not a la Natassia Kinski, but the pelts of foxes, slung over their shoulders, like the trappers of old.

There they were, complete with head, eyes, and fangs bared wide. Everywhere I looked, there were foxes, and everywhere I went, their eyes followed me. When you're only two years old, you're not quite sure whether such things are dead or alive. I could only draw marginal comfort from the fact that they were chained up by a clasp, so they couldn't get away. I was okay as long as they kept their distance.

However, there's something in a woman that gives her the false impression that a two-year-old isn't capable of standing on his own two feet. For this reason, as I look back on it now, I didn't have a chance. As "Trapper Joan" bent over to pick me up, her fox's head swung out wide and caught me right in the face! YEOOW!

I have observed, in over three decades of church-going

in hundreds of different churches, that Christians are united if not by denomination and communion, at least by fashion. Not that all true Christians wear only Brooks Brothers suits and Gucci shoes. Far from it. Generally speaking, Christians *dress up* to go to church on the Lord's Day.

This seems to be as true for High Church Anglo-Catholics as for Low Church Puritan Protestants, who are otherwise leery of symbols. It's as true for impoverished ghetto blacks as for peasants in Latin American villages. Christians observe a common custom of dressing up for worship on the Lord's Day.

To the best of my knowledge, no doctoral dissertation has ever been written on the history of Christian fashion. But there appears to be a long, long history to all of this.

From the year A.D. 215 we get our first detailed description of a Paschal Vigil.[22] Hippolytus, a teacher at Rome, writes:

> *At cockcrow prayer shall be made over the water. The stream shall flow through the baptismal tank or pour into it from above when there is no scarcity of water; but if there is a scarcity, whether constant or sudden, then use whatever water you can find. They shall remove their clothing. And first baptize the little ones; if they can speak for themselves, they shall do so; if not, their parents or other relatives shall speak for them. Then baptize the men, and last of all the women; they must first loosen their hair and put aside any gold or silver ornaments that they are wearing: let no one take any alien thing down to the water with them.[23]*

Now why were early Christians told to remove all their clothing and bring absolutely nothing with them into the baptismal waters? Two reasons:

1. It gives modern preachers a nice "R-rated" sermon illustration.

2. Baptismal nudity is a symbol. What does it mean?

Saint Paul alludes to the practice and explains its meaning: Put off your old nature which belongs to your former manner of life and is corrupt through deceitful lusts, and be renewed in the spirit of your minds, and put on the new nature, created after the likeness of God in true righteousness and holiness. (Ephesians 4:22-24)

The clothes that early Christians discarded as they stepped into the baptistery represented the "old nature," the former, sinful person that was about to be left behind. Saint Cyril writes that entering the baptismal waters in the nude was a symbol for a return to the innocence of the Garden of Eden. Baptism restores you to the state of Adam and Eve prior to the Fall.[24]

After being washed with the waters of baptism, the person would step out of the baptistery and be robed in a new, white gown — a symbol of the new person, the new creation, empowered to live the new life in Christ.

The Easter custom of a baptismal gown continues right down to the present. And, it continues among Christians everywhere who "dress up" on every Sunday — after all, every Sunday is a little Easter, and Easter is the Great Sunday.

This custom of dressing up for Sunday worship very nearly put my father in debtor's prison one year. As a ten-year-old, every Sunday morning I would put on my one sport-coat and head off to church. After services, I would hang it back up in the closet, where it would remain until the next Lord's Day.

One Sunday, while leaving church, the treasurer handed me a white envelope and told me to be sure to give it to my father. *Au contraire,* I put it in my breast pocket and promptly forgot about it. A week later, while putting the coat back on, I reached inside and discovered the envelope, remembering that I was supposed to have given it to him. Of course, by then, the bill collectors were knocking at our door.

Christians dress up for Lord's Day worship. This custom

is linked to baptism and it is linked to Easter. It is a symbol for the Easter message that is as vivid as any other.

Symbols, of course, stand for something. They are not the thing itself, but a sign of the thing. Whenever we confuse the religious sign with the thing that it signifies, we run into trouble, just like the driver who so admires a stop sign that he runs right through it. The logic of symbols tells us that what Christians wear (or don't wear) is not really the important thing. What's really important is what's going on underneath the symbols.

And what is going on — or should be going on — underneath the symbolism of dressing up for church? Six centuries before Christ, the prophet Ezekiel wrote of the New Covenant that would be fulfilled in the death and resurrection of Christ:

> I [the Lord] will take you from the nations, and gather you from all the countries, and bring you into your own land. I will sprinkle clean water upon you, and you shall be clean from all your uncleanness, and from all your idols, I will cleanse you. A new heart I will give you, and a new spirit I will put within you; and I will take out of your flesh the heart of stone and give you a heart of flesh.
>
> Ezekiel 36:24-28

Traditionally, the church has interpreted this as a prophecy foreshadowing baptism. How does baptism give you a new heart and a new spirit? The *waters* of baptism, of course, do not do this, anymore than does a new Easter outfit give you a new spirit. Both are symbols for something deep down inside — made possible only by the secret movement of the Holy Spirit.

This understanding of how symbols work gave rise to a famous definition of a sacrament. Saint Augustine defined a sacrament as: an outward and visible form of an inward and invisible grace.[25]

The sacraments are outward and visible forms of an

inward and invisible grace. We hope! There's nothing magical about them — although they are full of mystery. There's
nothing automatic about how they work, yet they bear
Christ's promise. There are no guarantees with sacraments
— yet they are means of grace for those who receive them
in faith.

In conclusion, I wish to share a couple of stories with
you. The first one comes from my seminary days. At Prince-
ton, they take the first-year students over to the Jersey shore
for an overnight. Since the only ocean shore I had ever visited
was in Washington State, I naturally (and foolishly) assumed
that the Jersey shore was just as wild and desolate. I packed
up my sleeping bag and various camping items, preparing
to "rough it." When I arrived at the luxury hotel I realized
that I had miscalculated — badly. At a formal dinner, I was
introduced to my professors, who, I am sure, to this day,
wonder about that student who came in a flannel shirt with
no tie.

The second story comes from my ministry at a country
parish in Northern Indiana. I had been there for several weeks
when I noticed that an elderly couple, who were regular
attenders, invariably wore the same outfits. The gentleman
always wore a 1940's suit (double-breasted, wide lapels,
stripes) along with button suspenders and a wide, flowery
tie. The wife always wore a purple hat with a feather, and
a magenta, wool suit, also right out of the 1940's. Rain or
shine, hot or cold, that's what they wore.

I was intrigued by this couple. Each week they would
chug up in their 1948 DeSoto. And each Sunday, they would
sit in the same pew. As they sat down, the folks behind them
would all re-adjust themselves so that they could see around
that feather. It was a delightful ritual to behold.

One night at the Deacons' meeting, we were discussing
needy families in the parish. I thought of this elderly couple, so strapped by a fixed income that they couldn't up-
date their wardrobe or means of transportation. When I

mentioned their names, the room erupted into peals of laughter. One of the deacons, a prosperous corn farmer explained why everyone was laughing: "That couple just happens to own five hundred acres of the best farmland in the county" (that's how Hoosiers describe millionaires).

The marvelous message of Easter is this: God loves us, whether we have flannel shirts or silk shirts, whether we have no tie or lots of ties. God loves us, whether or not we have a feather in our cap; God loves us, whether we own five hundred acres or no hundred acres.

The promise of the Covenant is that the redeeming love of God is there for each and every one of us. Whatever our circumstances in life, we are all very precious in the eyes of the Lord. To live under the shadow of God's wings is to be transformed by the power of the Holy Spirit. The New Covenant, ratified on this triumphant day, is God's eternal promise to dress us up on the inside — *so spiffily* — that we will show it all over on the outside!!

The Lord is risen! *He is risen indeed!*

Appendices

Further Reading in Covenant Theology

Brueggemann, Walter. *Genesis: A Biblical Commentary for Teaching and Preaching.* Atlanta, GA: John Knox, 1982.

Calvin, John. *Institutes of the Christian Religion.* Library of Christian Classics, Vols. 20-21. Ed. John T. McNeill, trans. Ford Lewis Brattles. Philadelphia: Westminster Press, 1960.

DeJong, Peter Y. *The Covenant Idea in New England Theology, 1620-1847.* Grand Rapids, MI: Wm. B. Eerdmans Publishing, 1945.

Holifield, Elmer Brooks. *The Covenant Sealed: The Development of Puritan Sacramental Theology in Old and New England, 1570-1720.* New Haven: Yale University Press, 1974.

Mendenhall, G. E. "Covenant." In *Interpreter's Dictionary of the Bible,* I: 714-23.

Moller, Jens G. "The Beginnings of Puritan Covenant Theology." *Journal of Ecclesiastical History* 14 (April 1963):46-67.

Rad, Gerhard von. *Genesis: A Commentary.* Old Testament Library. Philadelphia, PA: Westminster Press, 1961.

_____. *Old Testament Theology, I: The Theology of Israel's Historical Traditions.* Trans. D.M.G. Stalker. New York: Harper and Row, 1962.

Williams, J. Rodman. "The Covenant in Reformed Theology." *Austin Seminary Bulletin* 78 (March 1963):24-38.

Tools Useful in the Preparation of the Sermon Series

Craddock, Fred, *Preaching.* Nashville, Tennessee: Abingdon, 1985.

Davies, J. G., ed. *A Select Liturgical Lexicon.* Ecumenical Studies in Worship, 14. Richmond, VA: John Knox Press, 1970.

_____, ed. *The Westminster Dictionary of Worship.* Philadelphia: Westminster Press, 1972.

Harvey, Van A. *A Handbook of Theological Terms.* New York: Macmillan Co., 1964.

Interpreter's Dictionary of the Bible, 5 Vols. Ed. George A. Buttrick. Nashville: Abingdon Press, 1962.

The Jerome Biblical Commentary. Ed. Raymond E. Brown. Englewood Cliffs, NJ: Prentice-Hall, Inc. 1968.

Leon-Dufour, Xavier, ed. *Dictionary of Biblical Theology.* New York: Desclee Co., 1967.

Rahner, Karl, ed. *Sacramentum Mundi: An Encyclopedia of Theology.* New York: Herder and Herder, 1968.

_____, ed. *Encyclopedia of Theology: The Concise Sacramentum Mundi.* New York: Seabury, 1975.

Wakefield, Gordon S., ed. *Westminster Dictionary of Christian Spirituality.* Philadelphia: Westminster Press, 1983.

Lectionary Preaching Resources

Craddock, Fred, Ed. et alii. *Preaching the New Common Lectionary.* Nashville: Abingdon Press. (about $10.00 per volume)

Emphasis: A Preaching Journal for the Parish Pastor. C.S.S. Publishing Co., 628 South Main Street, Lima, Ohio 45804. ($20.00 per year)

Johnson, Sherman. *The Year of the Lord's Favor: Preaching the Three-Year Lectionary.* New York: Seabury Press, 1983.

Proclamation 3: Aids for Interpreting the Lessons of the Church Year. Philadelphia: Fortress Press. (about $3.00 per volume)

Sloyan, Gerard. *A Commentary on the New Lectionary.* New York: Paulist Press, 1975.

Notes

[1] J. Rodman Williams, "The Covenant in Reformed Theology." *Austin Seminary Bulletin* 78 (March 1963):24-38.

[2] New York: The Church Hymnal Corporation, 1983.

[3] The attributing of human emotions to God.

[4]*Indicates primary lesson(s) upon which homily is based. Roman Catholic psalm numbering appears first, Protestant numbering in parentheses.

[5] Count Hermann Keyserling. Cited in Joseph Epstein, *Divorced in America: Marriage in an Age of Possibility* (New York: E. P. Dutton, 1974).

[6]*National Geographic* 167 (January 1985):47.

[7] These homilies were originally preached less than 200 miles from Mount Saint Helens (Washington, USA). On 18 May 1980, the long-dormant volcano erupted with a violent explosion, causing widespread destruction and death. The event has since prompted many Pacific Northwest Christians to reflect upon their theology of creation.

[8] On January 28, 1986, just as this material was being prepared for publication, the news broke of the USA's first Space Shuttle disaster, killing all seven aboard.

[9] Bernhard W. Anderson, *Creation Versus Chaos: The Reinterpretation of Mythical Symbolism in the Bible* (New York: Association Press, 1967).

[10]*Theololgy of Nature* (Philadelphia: Westminster Press, 1980).

[11]*Ibid.,* p. 219

[12]*Lectures on Romans.* LW, 25 (St. Louis: Concordia Publishing House, 1972): pp. 243, 306-7.

[13] The distinction is usually made between natural law and supernatural or revealed law, which is known thorugh Christ and the church.

[14] John Calvin, *Institutes of the Christian Religion.* Library of Christian Classics, Vols. 20-21. Ed. John T. McNeill, trans. Ford Lewis Brattles (Philadelphia: Westminster Press, 1960): 2.7.1-9.

[15] Calvin, *Institutes* 2.7.10-11.

[16]*Institutes* 2.7.12-17.

[17] Presbyterian Church (U.S.A.), Book of Confessions, 6.038-9 (New York: Office of the General Assembly, 1985).

[18] E.g. Galatians 3:15, 17, 4:24; Ephesians 2:12; 2 Corinthians 3:6, 14; Acts 7:8.

[19] See also, Calvin, *Institutes* 2.11.4.

[20] Robert Daly, *The Origins of Christian Sacrifice* (Philadelphia: Fortress Press, 1978.)

[21] This sermon is based on the classic work by Swedish theologian, Gustav Aulin, *Christus Victor* (New York: Macmillan, 1969).

[22] The Vigil is the great celebration of Easter Eve or early Easter morn, when new persons, after a lengthy period of preparation, enter the church through Baptism.

[23]*Apostolic Tradition,* ed. Burton Scott Easton. Archon Books (Cambridge: Cambridge University Press, 1962), p. 45.

[24] "Mystagogical Catechesis." *The Works of St. Cyril of Jerusalem,* The Fathers of the Church, 64 (Washington, D.C.: Catholic University of America Press, 1970): pp. 161-62. Cyril writes: "Truly you bore the image of the first-formed Adam, who was naked in the garden and 'was not ashamed.' " He also draws a connection to Jesus hanging stripped upon the cross.

[25]*De catechizandis rudibus,* xxvi. 50.